Just Me

*Growing Up in
the 30s and 40s*

THOMAS MCCAVOUR

FriesenPress

Suite 300 - 990 Fort St
Victoria, BC, V8V 3K2
Canada

www.friesenpress.com

Copyright © 2021 by Thomas McCavour
First Edition — 2021

All rights reserved.

No part of this publication may be reproduced in any form, or by any means, electronic or mechanical, including photocopying, recording, or any information browsing, storage, or retrieval system, without permission in writing from FriesenPress.

ISBN
978-1-03-910265-1 (Hardcover)
978-1-03-910264-4 (Paperback)
978-1-03-910266-8 (eBook)

1. BIOGRAPHY & AUTOBIOGRAPHY, PERSONAL MEMOIRS

Distributed to the trade by The Ingram Book Company

In the Beginning

My name is John Seely and I would like to share some random thoughts with you about my life growing up in the 30s and 40s. Shall we begin?

Frankly I was not very happy about my rough introduction to the 20th century, after spending nine comfortable months in my mother's womb. I presume that I gave a loud cry when the doctor spanked me to clear the fluid from my lungs, but I do not remember all the details. There is no record of what I weighed. Who cares? I emerged from the hospital with all my body parts and an intact foreskin. I'm sorry about that one small detail, Abraham, but my sons Joseph and Erin have been properly mutilated. In reflection, I'm happy that the hospital, which was founded in 1897, had changed its name from the Rat Portage Jubilee Hospital to the Kenora General Hospital and has now morphed into the Lake of the Woods District Hospital. I would also have had difficulty explaining the rodent origin to my friends and family and the unfortunate naming of the town as Rat Portage. Fortunately, it changed. When the town was amalgamated with the neighboring towns of Keewatin and Norman in 1905, a committee in their wisdom, took the first two letters of each locality to create the new name of Kenora. They also could have grouped the two letters to spell Ranoke or Kerano, but I am happy with their first choice.

Kenora, Ontario is located about 200 km from the Manitoba boundary and was once claimed as part of the Province of Manitoba. There was long-lasting argument between the two provinces known as the Ontario Manitoba boundary dispute, and it was not settled in favor of Ontario, until 1889. Many of the local inhabitants felt that they would have been better of Manitoba.

....

I was not asked about the origin of my name but apparently heredity prevailed, and I was christened John, after my father's middle name and Claire after my uncle's first name. I liked the name John or Johnny as I was called as a youngster, but my uncle Claire Dunn's name was more suspect. I always had to explain that it was spelled with an "e" because it is the feminine derivation of Clara. I was then teased for having a girl's name. The name John is biblical and refers to one of Jesus Christ's twelve apostles. No one dared to tease me about that name.

My father Samuel John, who I will later identify as Esje, was raised in Saint John, New Brunswick. His grade 7 Report Card, which I somehow inherited, indicates excellent to good work, while his secondary and university years brought outstanding grades and gold medals. He had chosen a Civil Engineering education at the University of New Brunswick and following graduation in 1920, accepted apposition with the Fort Frances Pulp and Paper Company. In 1923 he moved to the small town of Kenora to build a new pulp and paper mill. At the age of twenty-four, Esje's testosterone was at work and he met and courted Barbara Dunn from the village of Keewatin. Since there was no road connection at the time, Keewatin was only accessible by train or by the Argyle ferry boat. Esje disliked commuting and proposed to Barbara. They were married in 1924 and resided in Kenora. My sister Marjory or Marj was born one year later and I followed, six years later.

In 1930 my father accepted a new job as Resident Engineer at the great Lakes Paper Company in Fort William, Ontario. He and Barbara, along with Marj and I, moved from Kenora to Fort William and lived in a house on John Street. Later that year, they bought a new home at 1416 Cuthbertson Place.

Fort William saw the establishment of sawmills and pulp and paper mills. Logs were harvested from the surrounding area, driven down local rivers and floated in booms along the shores of Lake Superior. Cheap electrical power was available from the upstream waters of the Kam River at Kakabeka Falls. The construction of railways enabled the western farmers to ship grain to the twin cities of Fort William and Port Arthur for transshipment by water on the Great Lakes. The Kam River and the shoreline of Thunder Bay was dotted with grain elevators. Between 1916 and 1935 the C. D. Howe Company built elevators in Vancouver, Saskatoon, Churchill, Port Arthur, Toronto and Prescott as well as Buenos Aires Argentina. Howe became the foremost grain elevator builder of his day. His straightforward and blunt personality and his ability to build elevators on time and at a fixed price, commended him to his customers, especially in Western Canada. Howe was a good friend of Esje and a frequent visitor to our home. Howe became a powerful Canadian Cabinet Minister of the Liberal party. Howe served in the governments of Prime Minister William Lyon Mackenzie King and Lois St. Laurent continuously from 1935 to 1957. He is credited with changing the Canadian economy from agriculture based to industrial. During the Second World War, his involvement in the war effort was so extensive, that he was nicknamed the Minister of Everything.

. . . .

My sister told me that in the 1920s our first home in Fort William was on John Street, but I can only remember growing up at 1416 Cuthbertson Place. Possibly that was because I had not been born. Cuthbertson Place was part of the Cuthbertson Estate and the movers and shakers in Fort William occupied the homes. There were only two houses on the even numbered south side of the street: a two-bedroom bungalow at 1414 and our three- bedroom two-story house at 1416. The houses were built in 1930 using uninsulated, brick-faced wood stud walls. The cavity between the brick and the interior wallboard was filled with sawdust, much to the delight of the local mouse population, who found it great for nesting. Cuthbertson Place was to be my home for the next twenty years. It is interesting to know about the origin and early history of Fort William. In the

1700s a fort was built on he Kaministiquia River. It was called Fort William and was used as a gateway to western Canada and as a fur trading outpost. Trade was with the local Chippewa Indians. With the passage of time, forestry became the main industry of Fort William. Saw- mills and pulp and paper mills were established.

· · · · · · · ·

Norm and Bertha Wheeler originally occupied the house at 1414. Norm was a chemical engineer employed at the time by the Great Lakes Paper Company. The Wheelers were good friends of my parents and that friendship lasted a lifetime. Norm was unfortunately injured during an explosion in the laboratory and lost the sight of one eye. He and Bertha moved to Espanola in the mid-1930s, where he managed and then became president of the KVP Company, producing specialty Kraft paper. Bert and Ethel Simpson became the next occupant of 1414 and would remain as neighbors for the next 30 years. Bert was the local manager of the LCBO and enjoyed drinking their products. After imbibing a little too much, Bert would stroll up and down the sidewalk between our houses singing and playing the ukulele. The performance was not appreciated by the neighbors.

The early north side residents were Jones, editor of the local Times Journal newspaper, Petroff, a shoe store owner, Sutton, a bank manager Martine, an estate manager; Barker, a teacher : Pearson, an architect; Berton, a harbormaster and Owen, a department store owner. In the 1940s, the homes of Spence, a doctor, Norton, a plumbing contractor; Moore, a Chrysler dealer; Wills, a teacher; Manly, an equipment manufacturer; Rourke, a retailer and Sproule, an architect, were built on the south side. This was not an ordinary street. It was occupied by the leaders of the city of Fort William. Was it considered snobbish and upper crust? Some may think so. In my youth, there was never any thought or action by my peers that made me feel different. Was I privileged? Yes, but it didn't matter. That it is not to say that there was no class prejudice at the time. The kids from the Island and from Simpson Street were unjustly considered to be inferior, because their fathers were usually blue-collar employees, working in the mills or elevators. Many were good friends, and some became famous.

JUST ME

· · · · · · ·

There were many events in my life that shaped my character. For instance, one was the practice of piling-on. The purpose of piling -on was to crush the person on the bottom. We were never successful in doing that, but the practice continued. If someone tripped or fell or if someone was tackled, you yelled pile-on and six to ten kids would throw themselves on top of the hapless victim. In reflection, was this just another form of physical bullying and mob action or was it just fun. I think that it was just fun since there was no malice or cruelty in our actions.

· · · · · · ·

I played strip poker up until the age of twelve. We usually played in nearby Vickers Park or in some secluded hideout where no one would see us. The purpose of the game was to strip your opponent of his clothes. Girls did not usually participate. For the benefit of those that do not know the rules of the game, I will explain. There are many variations, but we usually played five-card draw with the winner holding the best high cards. The winner of each game received an item of clothing from the losers. We finally persuaded Sally Waters to play with us. Sally was twelve years old and had matured early with two well developed breasts, which all the boys wanted to see. The trouble was that Sally always won. We ended up naked and she ended up with all of our clothing.

· · · · · · ·

My friend Roy Johnson cannot deny my story about the orange wrappers, because he is no longer with us. When we went to the outhouse at their Floral Beach cottage, we had to use orange wrappers instead of toilet paper when we went to the bathroom. Needless to say the orange wrappers were not particularly absorbent and only accomplished 95 percent of the job. Roy's dad had a well-paying job as the chief electrical engineer at the Great Lakes Paper Company, so there was no reason for this frugality, but those were the outhouse rules. My parents wisely brought their own toilet paper.

Tube radios were introduced into our home in the 30s, and I spent a good deal of time listening to the comedy and action shows. We didn't have television, tapes or video. They had not been invented. At noon, we listened to the Happy Gang. I can still remember the lyrics of their opening song.

Here we are, The Happy Gang is here,
Here we are, how do you do Here we
are to take away your troubles, With
a song of melody and cheer. We're
the hap, hap, happy gang.

In the afternoon it was the soaps, so named because they were all sponsored by soap companies. They included Road of Life, As the World Turns and Pepper Young's Family. I didn't get to listen to them unless I was at home sick, but my mother and grandmother were regular listeners. Comedy included Edgar Bergen, the ventriloquist and his puppet Charlie McCarthy. Of course, anybody could be a ventriloquist on radio, but he also appeared in the movies and on stage. Fibber McGee and Molly, George Burns and Gracie Allen were also favorites, along with the Aldrich Family and the opening yell from his mother – "Henreeee, Henry Aldrich."

For action, I listened to The Lone Ranger, The Shadow and Inner Sanctum. The house rule was that you could only listen to the programs if you had finished doing your homework. This was always a good incentive. Radio soap operas were born in the 1930s and lasted for the next three decades. It was the golden age of radio, and manufacturers of soap, food and tobacco products recognized that they could tap the huge market of stay-at-home housewives using this medium. It worked and there were hundreds of shows produced for afternoon radio. My mother and my grandmother were hooked. I became interested when I listened to the radio during my frequent sick leaves from school. I can remember Big Sister sponsored by

Rinso, The Guiding Light by Proctor and Gamble, Ma Perkins by Kellogg's All Bran and One Man's Family by Reynolds Tobacco. When I reluctantly returned to school, I would ask grandmother to recite what I had missed. In Thunder Bay you did not have a summer cottage: you had a camp. The word cottage was considered to be a snobbish term, only used by people from southern Ontario. Ned and Stella Johnson were good friends of my parents and they frequently invited our family to visit with them at their camp. The camp was a simple wood-frame building located at Floral Beach on the north shore of Thunder Bay on Lake Superior, about ten km east of Port Arthur. It was squeezed between the CPR railway track and the water. Automobiles had to be parked on the other side f the track and all the supplies had to be hauled on foot from the parking lot, over the tracks to the camp. The inconvenience explained the low cost of the land. There were hundreds of similar camps stretching to the far end of Thunder Bay, but none were so close to the railway track and most were accessible by automobile. Nevertheless, I spent many enjoyable days at the Johnson camp during the 1930s.

. . . .

Windmills were common at the time and were usually put to work by local farmers pumping water from a well. As a trained electrical engineer, Ned Johnson had reasoned that he could store the power generated by the wind in batteries and then use this stored energy to provide low voltage lighting for the camp. Eaton's sold a large amount farm equipment at the time in Western Canada. Ned ordered an Imperial Windmill from the Eaton's catalogue. His system had its limitations, but basically it worked. Eighty years later the concept was revisited, when wind power became part of the North American power grid and battery storage was put forward as a means of storing the unreliable energy source. We spent many hours playing badminton in a court at the back of the camp, but most of our time was spent in the waters of Thunder Bay. The beach was sandy and the water was shallow. The only problem was the proximity of the camp to the pulp and paper mill in Port Arthur. While the pulp logs were being transported to the mill in booms floating on the water, a good deal of bark was rubbed off. Depending on the wind, the bark floated on the water and ended up on Floral Beach. The mixture was enhanced by the proximity of the Port Arthur sewage plant, which discharged raw sewage directly into the waters of Thunder Bay. The environment was not a high priority in those days. The water was polluted.

Years later Ned Johnson built a beautiful camp in a remote wooded location on the shores of Lake Shebandowan. There were no train tracks to worry about and you could park beside the camp. The Shebandowan waters were unpolluted with an abundance of fish, which regularly appeared, pan-fried, on the breakfast table. The interior of the camp was finished with knotty pine lumber from trees that were growing on the site. There was also indoor plumbing with toilet paper instead of orange wrappers. My friend Roy Johnson inherited the property in the 1980s.

· · · · ·

I could never understand the practice of my mother and grandmother for putting out the wash on the clothesline in the middle of winter. The sheets, pillowcases, towels and clothing froze stiff in about five minutes. The wash would then flap around for several hours in big frozen chunks before I would be asked to bring it in. Needless to say, the clothespins and my fingers were frozen in the effort of pulling the frozen wash through the small and narrow clothesline door. I had to whack it, bend it and stack it like firewood before bringing it in the house. And carrying it down to the basement for it to thaw out. Then my mother or grandmother would run the material through the electric ironer to dry out and complete the process. I still do not understand why they persisted in this needless practice when it was a complete waste of time and electrical energy. They could have hung up the wash to dry in the basement, aided by the nearby furnace and providing humidity for the house. The humidity would have been welcome and the ironing unnecessary. My wife tells me that fresh air is good for the wash, Bah, humbug!

· · · · · · ·

JUST ME

I always looked forward to Halloween and had no idea that the ancient custom of remembering the dead had morphed into the entirely different North American custom of trick-or-treating, carving pumpkins into jack-o-lanterns, lighting bonfires, apple bobbing, playing pranks, visiting haunted attractions, telling scary stories and watching horror films. In many parts of the world, All Hallows' Eve included attending church services and lighting candles at the graves of the dead.

When my wife and I were in Mexico, we observed their custom for The Feast of the Dead. It evolved independently and coincidentally within days of our Halloween. They remember the dead by placing lighted candles, photographs, and the deceased persons' favorite food at the gravesite.

We didn't have ugly masks to wear like the children of today. My mother or my sister usually went to work with their cosmetics and painted my face. I preferred to go as the Lone Ranger wearing a simple black eye-mask, while one of my friends would go dressed as my Indian companion Tonto, complete with an Indian headdress and feather. AS we went from house to house, I would yell "Hi, ho, Silver away!" which was the name of the Lone Ranger's horse, while my friend Tonto would reply, "I am coming Kemo Sabe," which means scout.

I can remember one Halloween in particular. It had been a good night and I was returning home with a full bag of treats, when someone grabbed my bag in the dark and ran off with it. I always blame the theft on the Dutton gang, but others say it was our neighbor, Harry Scott. As an eight-year-old, I was devastated. I could not think of a worse disaster. Fortunately, my friends came to the rescue and each of them contributed part of their treats to make up the loss. This act of friendship has occurred many times during my life. When my wife miscarried during my final year at Queen's University, my schoolmates all donated blood to replace the blood transfusions that she required at the hospital.

· · · · · · ·

Like Linus with his blanket in the comic strip *Peanuts*, I had my Dacty. It was an old blue blanket, that provided me with great comfort as a young child. The problem was that I eventually became too old and I still would not give up my Dacty. I cannot remember the day that we separated, but it must have been traumatic We all need a Dacty when we are growing up. My daughter had a Mumpmick blanket as a baby and a Lucky the Cat pajama bag later on. My son Mike had a black and white dog called Ruff for his pajama bag, and my son Art had a brown pajama bag and a bear called Doreen. It was impossible for each of these children to go to sleep without them. I still miss my Dacty and hug my pillow instead.

. . . .

When I was growing up, we had an icebox to keep our food cool and fresh, so that it would not spoil. The icebox was located in the back porch so that the iceman could come and replace the ice without entering the kitchen. Another reason that it was in the back porch was because the drain pan was constantly overflowing. When the ice melted inside the refrigerator, it drained into a pan underneath. I was supposed to empty the drain pan every day, but sometimes I would forget, and it overflowed. I was to relive this event fifteen years later when Pat and I were first married. We lived in two rooms on the second floor of the Reeves residence in Niagara Falls. We had an icebox and I can still remember the screams from Mrs. Reeves, saying that the icebox was overflowing. I just never learned to empty the drain n on time. In Fort William and Port Arthur, the blocks of ice were cut in the winter when Boulevard Lake froze over. When the ice became quite thick, the cutters would then drill holes in the ice and insert big saws, to cut the ice into small blocks. Then they would take the blocks to an icehouse and cover them with left-over sawdust from the lumber mills. The sawdust acted like insulation and kept the ice from melting.

The iceman would deliver the blocks of ice in his truck. He usually came twice a week, and we would line up behind the truck, waiting for him to wash off the sawdust and trim the ice. He would wipe off the sawdust and then use an ice pick to shape the ice so that it would fit in the metal box at the top of the refrigerator. Then he would use metal tongs to grab hold of the block of ice so that he could carry it to the refrigerator. As soon as he was finished, we would pick up the small pieces of ice that he had left behind and suck them. There was nothing better on a hot summer day and it was free. Our cat, Toots, was usually with us and I would give her a small piece of ice that she could lick.

. . . .

I have come to the conclusion that comics are not always comical and that the funnies are not always funny. So why do I keep reading them? Is it entertainment or is it a form of escapism? I must admit that I do laugh when I read *For Better or for Worse* by Lynn Johnston because it depicts the real-life experiences of living with cats, dogs, turtles, birds and goldfish; marriage to the love of your life and a career. the real-life experiences of raising our children along with I think it is my favorite. I also read contemporary strips such as *Dilbert* by Scott Adams, which is a cubicle eyed view of bosses, business meetings, management fads, and other workplace afflictions. Having experienced the life of working as an employee of a large company and also being the boss of my own company. I support Dilbert's principles and find the strip amusing. I also read *Sherman's Lagoon by* Jim Toomey, *Tina's Groove* by Rina Piccolo and *Retail* by Norm Feuti, Blondie, created by Chic Young in the early 1930s is my favorite. The comic is the life story of Blondie and Dagwood Bumstead, their children Alexander and Cookie, their dog Daisy, their neighbors Tootsie and Herb Woodley, Mr. Beasley the postman, Dagwood's boss Julius Caesar Dithers and wife Cora, and an annoying neighborhood kid named Elmo Tuttle. This comic strip reminds me of my own life experiences.

The comics of today are very different from the action comics that I read as a child in the 1930s. During the week, comic strips appeared in the Fort William Times Journal, and on the weekend, there was a whole section of the Star Weekly devoted to comics. I also bought comic books at ten cents each and then traded them with my friends. It was always a difficult decision whether to invest in candy or comic books, to satisfy my taste buds or to satisfy my mind. Comic books were a collection of comic strips put together to create a single short story in twelve to sixteen pages. Many of the comics were actually adventure stories, including *Buck Rogers, Flash Gordon, Batman, Wonder Woman and Captain Marvel.*

I particularly liked *Superman,* disguised as Clark Kent, a reporter working at the Daily Planet, who derived his great powers of strength and air flight from the mineral krypton, from his birthplace on the planet Krypton. *Superman* was always busy catching the bad guys and rescuing his girlfriend, Lois Lane. Then there was Spiderman who could catch the bad guys in his web and climb buildings like a spider. This type of comic strip gradually disappeared and was replaced by strips such as *Peanuts* by Charles Schulz in the 1950s. Dick Tracy and his amazing cast of characters was a good read. I was introduced to B. O. Plenty, his wife Gravel Gertie and their daughter Sparkle Plenty; Orphan Annie with her dog Sandy and her father Daddy Warbucks; Maggie and her husband Jiggs who like corned beef and cabbage.; Mutt and Jeff; Popey, who derived great strength by eating spinach with his sweetheart Olive Oil and their baby Sweetpea; and the Little Kings, are all strips that are now gone, thus proving that comic writers and comic strips are mortal. Some of the comic writing was prophetic about the technology of today. I think of Dick Tracey's wristwatch, which he also used as a phone, Buck Rogers introduction of space travel for humans and Flash Gordon's use of missiles and rockets. Today there are collectors of comic books and conventions for comic boo collectors who continue the tradition. Will comics continue to entertain us? I think so, but probably not in print form. I still read and enjoy the comic strips.

. . . .

There were four theatres in Fort William, named the Orpheum, the Royal, the Capitol and the Fort, The Orpheum was the grand old theatre, built like an opera house with a curved balcony and boxes at the sides. It was similar to the Royal Alexander Theatre in Toronto, but smaller in scale. The Capitol was the modern theatre, while the Royal and the Fort were pedestrian. When I was nine or ten, I would go to the Royal Theatre on Saturday mornings at a reduced price. We would line up outside the theatre on Victoria Avenue, waiting to get in and then, after fueling up with popcorn, we would spend the morning watching cartoons, the news, sometimes a serial story followed by the feature movie. There was a continuous stream of movies coming out of Hollywood at the time. I was hooked on Westerns. There were Traditional Westerns featuring actors like John Wayne, Ken Maynard, Jimmy Stewart and Erol Flynn. There were Singing Cowboy Westerns featuring Roy Rogers, Gene Autrey and Tex Ritter; as well as Comedy Westerns with Stan Laurel, Oliver Hardy and Charles Laughton. Ladies also played an important part in Westerns and included Olivia de Haviland, Claudette Colbert and Marlene Dietrich. There were other action movies. One of my favorites was Tarzan of the Apes, starring Johnny Weissmuller and Maureen O'Sullivan. It was based on the book written by Edgar Rice Burroughs and was produced in many forms. I also learned how to imitate the Tarzan yell as he swung through the trees by holding on to the hanging vines. I tried to imitate Tarzan by launching myself on the clothesline from the laundry chute. I managed to pull down the clothesline. As I grew older, my taste for movie entertainment changed and I saw different types of movies at the Orpheum and Capitol theatres including musicals, comedies, mysteries and adventures. I was hooked on the movies.

· · · · · · · ·

Canadians wear cold weather underwear in winter and some even wear it year-round. When I was growing up, we all wore long johns or thermal underwear, and although they kept you warm in the winter, there were some disadvantages. There has been some debate about why the underwear was called long johns, but the consensus seems to be that they were named after the boxer John L. Sullivan, who wore long johns when he was fighting in the ring. There is a minority who argue that the name is linked to the problem of going to the toilet, which is referred to as the john. It is agreed that the name is not linked to a prostitute's customer, who also is referred to as a john. I will side with the toilet gang and therein lies a problem. The underwear was in one piece, buttoned down the front, so that you could put it on. Females were at a distinct disadvantage. There was a fly opening at the front for males to urinate and a rear flap at the back for bowel movements. The flap at the back was a problem. You could not get the darn flap unbuttoned and re-buttoned when you went to the toilet. Imagine having your arm around your back fumbling with the buttons. The flap opened horizontally with the buttons at the top. Recognizing the problem, the manufacturer eventually created a flap that opened vertically with fewer buttons. This was great for right-handed people but not for lefties. It took a Canadian by the name of Myles Stanfield to solve the problem. He produced thermal underwear in two pieces and had the foresight to patent the design. His company became one of the major manufacturers of underwear in North America. Myles son Robert became the premier of Nova Scotia and the leader of the Federal Conservative party. His Maritime charisma could not compete with Pierre Trudeau and Trudeaumania, so he remained in opposition for the remainder of his political life. My wife, who actually wore long johns as sleepwear in winter, tells me that her Grandpa Martin wore his long john all year long. I trust that her mom was able to wash them once in a while.

· · · · · · ·

I really love blueberries, particularly if they are in a pie. I started picking and eating blueberries at an early age, when I was visiting my grandmother in Keewatin. They were low-bush berries growing among the rocky area s behind her home. Local Indian children would come by the house selling a honey pail full of blueberries for twenty-five cents. When I grew older, I used to pick blueberries near our camp at Amethyst Harbor. You had to look out for bears because they enjoyed the berries as much as I did. In recent years, my wife and I picked high-bush blueberries at nearby Fernwood Farms. This was much easier than picking low-bush berries. There was such an abundance of fruit that you could sit comfortably on a stool. milking the clusters of berries on the bushes.

· · · · · · ·

Trading cards had been practiced since the late 1800s. but it was not until the 1930s that the manufacturers of gum started to insert them in packages of bubble gum. It was a smart way to sell more gum. There were baseball cards, comic cards and war cards. I collected bubble gum war cards. I bought the gum at the corner store and they cost one cent each. The cards were seventy-five mm by one hundred mm, made out of paperboard or thick paper, with an image on one side and an explanation of the image on the other side. I remember that my cards depicted gory scenes from the Japanese Manchurian war in the early 1930s. I actually paid very little attention to the image or the description. I was just interested in collecting more cards. I collected, traded and played games with the cards. One of the games was to stand and flip a card towards a wall. The card that landed closest to the wall or leaning against the wall won the game. The opponents then had to forfeit their cards.

· · · · · · ·

Marbles were often mentioned in Roman literature and there were many examples of marbles being used in early Babylonia and ancient Egypt. The games were played with a variety of materials including nuts, stones and molded clay. My marbles were made from glass formed into small balls. I kept my marbles in a bag with a drawstring. As soon as the winter snow melted, I was outdoors playing marbles with my friends. The most popular game was similar to curling or lawn bowling. The players would take turns rolling their marble to a designated target and the closest to the target would win all of the marbles. We played the game at every opportunity including recess at Isabella School. Nothing was more embarrassing than to drop your bag of marbles on the classroom floor and watch the marbles roll all over the room to the amusement of your friends.

The expression "You have lost your marbles," was derived from the game meaning that you had lost your senses.

· · · · · · ·

I guess that at age eight, I was the last member of my friends that still believed in Santa Claus. My friend Bob Sutton had advised me that it was my parents that filled up my Christmas stocking, which was always hung by the fireplace. I refused to believe it and I had proof. In 1938, long before television computers and fax machines, important messages were sent by telegram. The message was first received at the railway telegraph station. It was typed on tape, glued to a blank telegram, phoned to the recipient and then hand-delivered by a messenger on a bicycle. On Christmas Eve 1938, I received a telegram, with some creative help from my parents, sent from Sant Claus. It said that he was on his way and that I would receive most of the things that I had asked for in my letter, as long as I remained a good boy. I couldn't sleep that night and at four in the morning I could hear Santa's sleigh on the roof of our house. I sneaked into bed with my sister and told her about it. She went along with my parent's deception and confirmed that she had heard it as well, turned over and then went back to sleep. I spent the next two hours, wide awake watching the clock and waiting to go downstairs to collect my loot. Sure enough, at six in the morning I was awake and ran downstairs. My stocking had been stuffed and there was further evidence that Santa had been there. The glass of milk that I had left for him was empty and there were a few shortbread crumbs left on the plate. My father had a lump of coal in his sock as punishment for telling a lie.

While I was thinking and writing about Santa Claus, I followed a debate on the Internet dealing with the question "Should children believe in Santa Claus?' In the debate, sixty-one percent said yes and thirty-nine percent said no. I have reprinted the following 'yes" argument and agree with the unknown source.

I have heard many arguments against the tradition of Santa Claus. During that time, I have never encountered a single individual who had been hurt by the tradition of Santa, no one has embarked on a life of deception and crime, no-one has expressed ill-will toward their lying parents and no-one has lost true religious convictions as a result of their childhood belief in Santa Claus. Only joy and fond childhood memories seem to result from this belief. To those who believe it is wrong to lie to a child, I would ask you to consider the nature of childhood; it is a time of imagination. No rational person would argue against the fostering of imagination in children. Educators encourage imagination. It's odd that many who oppose Santa on this premise allow their children to read and watch works of phantasy, some less than healthy. Children also learn through play. It plays an important part in social interactions; plus, it's just plain fun. Even adults love to play; we have sports, fishing, crafts and a variety of other things, the best of which include our children. Santa is the ultimate play for child and parent. To those who think that Santa distracts from the true meaning of Christmas, I respect your conviction. As a Christian I hold sacred the true meaning of Christmas. Many say that Santa is a pagan superstition. Our image of Santa has been influenced by history. Let me point out that Christianity has a long history of replacing pagan festivals and traditions with a Christian alternative. Christian churches now offer fall festivals as an alternative to Halloween. With regard to Christmas, we saw no conflict in attending our Christmas Eve worship service, going home to prepare for Santa's visit and reading the Christmas story before going to bed. As a final note, Jesus was fond of teaching in parables. Parables are simple stories that have a deeper meaning. The deeper truth may not be understood immediately, but time brings a greater understanding of the simple child-like story. I like to think of Santa as a parable, not a Biblical parable but a parable, nonetheless. Santa is a wonderful opportunity to teach values that will be important later in life.

So, I will continue to support the tradition and hope that many generations of my family to follow, will also support the tradition.

. . . .

We didn't have a Fort William Santa Claus parade when I was growing up; we had something better. and it was held indoors where it was nice and warm. The occasion was the Great Lakes Paper Company Christmas Party . It was held on a Saturday and all the employees attended along with their children. It was held in a cavernous structure called the paper storage warehouse, where all the finished rolls of newsprint were stored, waiting for shipment by boat to newspapers in Chicago. Everyone sat in temporary bleachers, enjoying the warm-up entertainment and carol singing, while waiting for Santa to arrive. Santa would finally appear riding on a huge lift truck, which was used for moving the rolls of paper and was now loaded with presents for the kids. We all received a bag of candy and a gift. Each family left with a frozen turkey. Of course, I knew that it was not the real Santa Claus. It was actually our family friend Dan Mavery. His son Tony, who was two years older than me, told me the secret.

THOMAS MCCAVOUR

·······

I never really paid much attention to Grandma Dunn's face or any other face for that matter, except my own. At any rate Grandma Dunn was constantly putting cosmetics on her face to cover her mysterious skin disease. Grandma slept in the bedroom next to mine and when she wasn't looking, I would sneak into her room to check out the cosmetics. Her top right-hand drawer was full of pills, powders and ointments. She even had some Carter's Little Liver Pills, a heavily advertised patent medicine which was supposed to cure headaches, constipation dyspepsia and biliousness. Years later, the company was forced to remove liver from their name. From time to time, Grandma Dunn would announce that she was going to take a train trip to Winnipeg and stop off at Keewatin to see her son Claire and his wife Molly. Actually, I knew that she was going to visit her dermatologist for gold treatments. The medical profession of the time was experimenting with gold as a means of reducing inflammation, as well as the cosmetic to remove wrinkles, age spots and other skin damage. I have no idea whether the gold treatments worked, and I suspect that Grandma Dunn had skin cancer.

·······

I like to whistle, my mother liked to whistle and my grandson likes to whistle. My friend Bob and my sister couldn't whistle. You can either whistle or you can't. You either liked it or you hated it. There are two kinds of whistling. You can use your lips alone or your lips and teeth. It helps if you have a good gap in your teeth. I am mainly a lip whistler, but I can also whistle with both lips and teeth.

Some people have made a career out of whistling. Roger Whittaker, a South African entertainer, is an excellent whistler and singer. I prefer *Amazing Grace and If I Were a Rich Man* from the play Fiddler on the Roof, while my mother preferred *How Great Though Art*. Whistlers have their favorite tunes. *Whistle While You Work* was a song introduced in the

Disney movie, Snow White and the Seven Dwarfs. It depicts the happiness that the dwarfs obtained by working. I think that is a good message. It is said that if you whistle, you are a happy and inwardly contented person. I think in my case, the observation is correct. I like to whistle and I'm also happy.

Just whistle while you work
And cheerfully together we can tidy up the place
So hum a merry tune
It won't take long when there's a song to help you set the pace
And as you sweep the room
Imagine that the broom Is someone that you love
And soon you'll find you're dancing to the tune
When hearts are high the time will fly
So whistle while you work.

Chamber pots, or pots de chambre in French, were used in ancient Greece at night, in the absence of indoor plumbing. They have since also evolved into bedpans and urinals. We used chamber pots at our summer cottage at Amethyst to avoid long treks in the dark to the outdoor privy. The porcelain pots were bowl shaped with a handle and often a lid. They were usually located under the bed and out of sight. The pots were very useful for boys to urinate in, while girls found them to be quite noisy. Bowel movements were more difficult, involving balance, aim and manual dexterity. I do not recommend this use, unless there is no other alternative. A miss is a disaster. Since we did not have a chambermaid, the youngest member of the family, namely yours truly, was delegated to collect the pots and carry them out to our two-hole privy. I dreamed of having a younger sibling who would inherit the job. Life has now come full circle, since I now have to use a urinal for my own incontinence.

· · · · · · ·

When the Spence house was built next door to our home on Cuthbertson Place, we said goodbye to the potato wars that were a favorite childhood activity. Our battlefield was gone. The excavators had arrived with two large draft horses and a clam shovel. This was before the backhoes of today. It was the way all types of excavation were carried out. After staking out the boundaries of the house for the basement, the horses would pull the clam shovel across the ground, fill it up and then deposit it on the far side. Back and forth they went, and the excavation became deeper and deeper, At the end of the day, the excavation was six feet deep and all traces of our war trenches and remnants of the spud wars had disappeared. I was annoyed with my parents for selling the property and the Spence family for building their house.

• • • • • • •

Despite the fact that my parents had forced me to attend swimming lessons at the YMCA, I never mastered the overhead crawl. I could dive and I could swim using the sidestroke, but I could not do the overhead crawl, which is the basic stroke for long distance swimmers. In fact, I still cannot do the overhead crawl. We had a cottage at Amethyst Harbor on the East Bay shores of Lake Superior. Children's swimming races were held at various times and on one occasion there was a race on East Bay. This was familiar territory for me. I had swum there many times We had to dive in at Norton's dock and then swim across the bay. I entered and won the race. One of the judges remarked that it was the first time that the race had ever been won by anyone using the sidestroke.

• • • • • • •

My grandfather was the manager of the Maple Leaf Milling Company in Keewatin and lived in a house on a nearby rocky hill. A highway and a railway separated the house from the harbor on the Lake of the Woods. The Argyle II ferry was moored at the dock on the harbor. A spur track from the railway led to the flour mill. My uncle Claire Dunn and his wife Sally had a home a short distance east on the highway. Claire was a tall and quiet man. Sally was a miniature and was severely crippled with arthritis. They would remain childless. Claire worked at the milling company. I owe my middle name to him. I always thought that it was a sissy name, but now I don't mind, particularly after I found out that it means "bright". The rear part of grandfather Dunn's property was rocky, and I spent hours of my time quarrying rock and then crushing it to make roads for my toy trucks. It was a great place to play. I could even pick blueberries and catch snakes to torment my sister and mother.

There was no running water at the Dunn home. They relied on a well, grey water was flushed down the hill and waste from an indoor toilet was collected indoors. The toilet had a conventional seat, a lid and a large removeable pail. The contents would be sprinkled with lime to kill the smell and keep down the flies. Men with a horse-drawn honey wagon would come once a week to empty the pail. If there were a large number of visitors at the house, the pail would be quite full. I had no idea how the men could lift the heavy pail and remove it from the house without a spill. They never tripped and fell. It would have been an unforgettable sight and an unbelievable smell.

· · · · · · ·

Fort William was originally laid out with front streets and back lanes serving the houses. As a result, homes were built wit separate garages at the back, accessible from the lane. Unlike the subdivisions of today, this resulted in a very pleasing residential area with no garages or driveways at the front. Garbage was picked up and deliveries of milk, ice, bread and groceries were made from the back lane; it was a homeowner's responsibility to maintain the section of the lane behind their house. There were problems with laneways behind vacant lots, laneways behind sick homeowners or inconsiderate homeowners who did not take care of their portion of the lane. The removal of snow was a major problem, since there was no place to pile it. Normally friendly neighbors stopped talking to each other, because one or the other had not done their job. My father finally ended the strife by forming a committee to assess all of the neighbors and have the lane cleared by a contractor.

· · · · · · ·

I worried a great deal about the size of my head when I was growing up. Children are very conscious of their appearance at that age and want to conform. It seemed to me that my head was unusually large. When I looked at a group photograph, I would check to see if anyone had a head that was the same size or hopefully larger than mine. No Luck! All of my friends had smaller heads. I am satisfied with the size of my head now. I guess that I just grew into it.

· · · · · · ·

My parents insisted that I wear breeches and knee socks, similar to those worn in European countries. The fact that wearing knee breeches died out at the end of the nineteenth century did not seem to make any difference. My parents argued that if they were suitable for the Royal Canadian Mounted Police and also equestrians, they were suitable for an eight-year-old. I argued that I did not ride a horse and all my friends wore long pants. They merely replied that it was very suitable for a young boy to wear breeches in the wintertime and that they were warmer than long pants. I prayed for an early end to winter.

· · · · · · ·

My father had two table manner edicts. The first was hat you should not eat with your elbows on the table and the second rule was that you could not use your finger to push food on to your fork. As a small child seated on the same height of chair as an adult, it is physically difficult to eat without putting an elbow on the table. My father did not agree and would recite: *Get your elbows off the table. This is not a horse's stable.*

At other times he would merely holler Elbows! The fact that the rhyme did not make any sense made little difference. I worked out my own frustrations in married life by reciting the same rhyme to my children and they in turn took out their revenge on their own children. With regard to the second packing finger rule, I would argue that we are all born with a packing finger and God or whoever else was in charge, wanted us to use it for eating. I thought it was a very stupid rule. "How else are you going to eat your peas; with a fork?" I argued, "Do you stab them one at a time?" I was, of course, overruled by Esje, but I have worked out my frustration by applying the same rule to my own children. Do "the sins of the fathers" apply here? *Watch your packing finger.*

· · · · · · ·

In addition to worrying about the size of my head, I also worried about the appearance of my hair, particularly when I was in high school. I couldn't pass a mirror without checking it out. I combed it, brushed it, and washed it. I did everything but curl it, since it was already naturally curly. When I was in public school, they called me Blondie, because my hair was always bleached by the sun in the summer and later turned brown in the winter. None of my friends seemed to worry about their hair except me. I used a variety of different hair oils. My favorite was Brylcreem. I liked their radio ditty.

Brylcreem, a little dab will do ya
Brylcreem, you look so debonair.
Brylcreem, the gals will pursue ya.
Simply put a little in your hair.

When I was courting Pat in high school my hair was curly and fluffed up. I would spend a long time getting it just right for the date. As soon as I arrived at Pat's home, Pat's sister Dolly would sneak behind me and mess up my hair. I hated Dolly then, but have learned since, to love her. I still have a full head of hair with a slightly bigger forehead, but no bald spots. My sister and I share the same DNA and she also had a full head of hair. I think that it must come from my mother because all of the males on both sides of the family were either bald or slightly bald. Maybe we are illegitimate?

· · · · · · ·

Grant Murphy owned a coal company and was one of the richest men in Fort William. He lived nearby on Selkirk Street in a huge house surrounded by stone walls with iron gates and railings. Grant was a short, thickset man with a high-pitched voice. I thought that his wife Dolores looked like a movie star with her blond hair and beautiful clothes. Grant used to advertise on the local CKPR radio station with a vocal group, singing the following ditty:

Burn Murphy's coal, it's the best, it's the best.
You'll feel as warm as a bird in it's nest,
When you need heat, there is nothing can beat,
Murphy's coal, Murphy's coal, it's the best.

We burned Murphy's coal at home, and I will tell you more about it when I write about taking care of our furnace.

. . . .

Unlike the warm air systems of today our house was heated with hot water that circulated through a system of steel pipes and cast-iron radiators. The system worked because our house was always warm even on the coldest day of winter. Our furnace used Murphy's coal and I was responsible for keeping it continuously supplied with coal, shoveled from an adjacent coal bin, removing the clinkers of fused coal and ash that formed on the grate, shaking down the coal bed and removing the remaining ash from the base of the furnace.

The Sutton family had a coalfired hot air furnace to heat their house and my friend Bob was the stoker. The furnace looked like a huge octopus with pipe ducts leading off in all directions to heat the house. I envied the Johnson family, who had a hot water system with the coal fed into the furnace by an automatic stoker with an auger that conveyed the coal from the bin to the furnace. The Sutherland family, quite naturally, had an electric boiler, since electricity was their business. I tended the coal furnace for about 10 years before Esje switched to oil. It had been an excellent learning experience It taught me about responsibility.

JUST ME

. . . .

When I wrote the Keyhole novel. I had a chapter describing the spud wars and the participation of Toots the cat. Let me quote from Chapter Seven.

> *"Peace cannot be achieved through violence.*
> *It can only be attained through understanding."*
> *Ralph Waldo Emerson*

Amanda looked through the keyhole and saw one of the strangest things. TC and some friends were in a field throwing something at some boys on the other side of the field. it looked like they were throwing small potatoes at each other. Amanda immediately reported this event to TC.

'What was going on, TC?"

"Oh, you were watching the spud war. Our gang was fighting the Horner gang. We had a spud war each fall after Mr. Agar dug up his crop of potatoes. He was only interested in harvesting large potatoes and didn't care about the small ones."

"I still do not understand, TC. What is a spud war?"

"Okay. Let me explain. Actually, it was not a real war. It was a game that we played. It was a lot of fun."

TC settled back in his rocking chair. He had left his pipe in the house.

"Do you want me to get your pipe, TC?"

"No thank you Amanda. Your mother says that I should not smoke so much."

He laughed and winked.

"I always do what she tells me. Okay, here's the story. When I was growing up there were only two houses on our side of the street. The rest of the property was used for growing potatoes. In the spring Mr. Agar, the dogcatcher, would bring a horse and a plough and turn over the soil so that he could plant potatoes. There were no insecticides at the time and in the summer, he would get us to pick bugs off the potato plants. They were big orange-colored bugs that ate the leaves. He would pay us two cents for each soup can, full of bugs. Then we would take the money down to the candy store to buy licorice, bubble gum and black balls.

Mr. Agar also told us that we could have all of the small leftover potatoes or spuds after he dug up the big potatoes in the fall. We also had to clean up any mess that we made." "So why did you have a war using spuds?" Amanda asked.

"Well, there was always a war going on in some part of the world when I was growing up and boys, being boys, we always played with guns and toy soldiers. The movies of the day were usually about cowboys and Indians and always involved fighting. A conflict between the Japanese and the Chinese, called the Manchurian War had just ended, but there were still pictures of this conflict on our bubble gum cards and in our comic books. I guess that we were just as bad in our day as you are today, watching violence on the television and in the movies. 'After Mr. Agar had harvested his potatoes, my friends and I took over the field and collected all the small spuds. We invited the Horner gang, who lived on the next street to come over and help us."

"Why did you call them the Horner gang?"

"There were nineteen children in the Horner family, and they were all born one year apart. So, there were always considered to be a gang with enough kids from one family to fight a war. "After we had gathered up the small potatoes, we would get shovels and dig trenches in the earth, because that is what you did to fight a war. We dug our trenches on one side of the property and the Horner gang dug trenches on the other side. Then we would create a bomb shelter and a hospital by widening one end of the trench and covering it with boards and sheet metal. Next, we would have a war meeting with the Horner hang to make up some war rules for throwing potatoes at each other.

"First, you had to stand up in the trench to throw a potato and you could not leave the trench. Second, if you were hit on the head by a potato, you were dead, and you were no longer in the game. Dying was rare. Third, if you were hit anywhere on the body, you were wounded and had to go to the hospital. This meant that you could not play until the next round. Reporting a hit was based on an honor system. The winner of the war was the last man standing." Amanda was getting interested. "So, what was a round?" "A round, TC replied, was when you ran out of potatoes. Then we would declare a truce, so that we could gather up the potatoes for the next round. . "Did Toots get involved in the spud wars?"

"Toots loved the spud wars. She would be in the trench helping us. Whenever a potato landed in the trench, she would pounce on it and then bring it to me. For her, it was better than catching mice." "Did your gang or the Horner gang ever win a war?" "No," TC replied.

"That never happened. When it got dark, we were usually tired and we would just declare a truce, shake hands and agree to fight another day."

'Did you ever fight in a real war TC?" . "No, I did not, Amanda. I was very fortunate. I was too young to fight in a war. I was nine years old when the Second World War started and fifteen when it ended. I hope that in your lifetime, that you never go to war. I do not believe that disputes should be settled by fighting or having wars. I believe that disputes can and should be resolved by discussion and compromise. I hope that you will not only share, but also practice those beliefs."

· · · · · · · ·

My family rented a North Bay Amethyst cottage from the Presbyterian church for two months in the summer. It was quite large and normally used as a retreat by the church. It was a great place to live. There was no running water at the cottage and no electricity. The cottage was located on a height of land about 30 feet above the bay with a long stairway running from the cottage to the water. One of my chores was to carry two pails of drinking water from the base of the hill, where the pump was located, up the stairs to the cottage. My other chore was to split wood for the stove and the fireplace. I preferred splitting wood. Every day my mother would give me a shopping list and I would head off to the general store located on South Bay on my bike. I looked forward to these trips because I was usually given some money to buy myself a treat. It was also an opportunity to meet with my friends from the other cottages. In the '40s, my friend Jack Doran's parents rented a cottage on South Bay and looked after the store. There was a creek near our cottage and my friend Mick and I, as embryonic civil engineers, would spend hours creating a dam at the outlet, before it emptied into the bay. There were tadpoles and frogs that occupied the pond available for catching. We also discovered an underwater source of clay in the otherwise sandy bottom of North Bay, which allowed us to create all manner of bowls and figurines.

We had a two-hole outhouse at our North Bay Amethyst cottage. It was not built for personal companionship; it was just a practical solution for little kids with little bums and big adults with big bums. There was a big hole and a little hole. Every little kid knows that if there is only one big hole, you have to sit forward so you don't fall in. It is also very difficult to wipe your behind. One of the signs of maturity is graduating and moving over to the big hole.

I guess that if the two-hole outhouse did not exist, there would be no need for the joking remark about the voice from below saying, "Would you please move over, I'm working down here."

· · · · · · ·

One of my jobs was to shovel the sidewalks in the winter. The trouble was that winter in Fort William started in November and ended in March. I did not have to shovel the backyard, where the car was parked, but I did have to shovel all the sidewalks including the back steps, the sidewalk between our house and the neighbor, the front steps and then the front sidewalk out to the street. I calculated that I had to shovel seventy-five feet of sidewalk while my friend Mick Sutton shoveled only thirty feet. It was unfair. Mick's older brother, George, who did not believe in any form of exercise, argued that shoveling was unnecessary, since the snow would all melt in the spring. George later became a lawyer. I particularly thought that our neighbor should shovel half of our shared sidewalk. Out of spite, I only made it one shovel wide and threw the snow on his side.

· · · · · · ·

You can make a very good tractor by using an elastic and a wood-spool. First you get a spool from your mother's or your grandmother's sewing basket. If it has some thread remaining, cut it off and then hide the thread in the garbage. Then take a kitchen paring knife or a jackknife and serrate or make v-notches along the rim of the spool. Find two wooden matchsticks and a elastic band. Cut a matchstick notch in one end of the spool to hold the matchstick in place. Cut one matchstick in half, tie one end of the elastic around it, thread it through the spool and then loop it around the other matchstick. Wind the elastic up by turning the match round and round, Place the spool on a flat surface and you were ready for racing.

While the boys were busy with their spool tractors, their female peers used spools for more practical purposes. Spool knitting was easy.

By tapping four or five headless nails into the end of the spool and then threading and looping wool around the nails, they could create a continuous hollow string. The strings could then be stitched together to make hats, doilies, wristbands and floral shapes.

· · · · · · ·

We did not build igloos like the Eskimo, we had our own method. There was always plenty of snow at my home in Fort William. During the period from November to March, we would get up to six feet of snow. The problem was that there was no place to store the snow. The piles just got higher and higher. The biggest pile was in my own backyard. Men from the Great Lakes Paper Company would come and shovel out our back driveway and they piled the snow between our garage and the house. The pile could be as high as the garage. As soon as the pile was high enough, we would tunnel in and start to enlarge a cave-like space inside the snow pile. We removed the snow by crawling through the tunnel, pulling a sleigh and throwing the snow on the newly cleared driveway. My parents were not impressed with the resulting mess. Afterhours of work, we had created a space, large enough to accommodate two or three kids and high enough that we could stand up. As the space was enlarged the igloo became weaker and the snow roof thinner, leading to its eventual, collapse. This was an introduction to my structural engineer career.

· · · · · · ·

We didn't build snowmen; we built forts. The snow had to be just right, so that it would stick together when you rolled it up like a jelly roll. When we then stacked the rolls up to make a wall, about chest high, so that you could lob a snowball at the enemy. Mick and I built forts on either side of the street, so you needed to have a good throwing arm. We took great care in making the snowballs. They had to be about the size of an orange, so that you could grab them in your mitt ready for throwing. The best ammunition was an ice ball. We made the snowballs, wet them and let them freeze overnight. During an attack, the enemy would run at your fort in an effort to smash down your walls and grab your snowballs. The snowballs would fly in all directions, accompanied by our whoops and screams, until one side or the other won the battle. It had been agreed, that if the Horner gang ever attacked, we would join forces to defend against a common enemy. They never attacked.

· · · · · · ·

The Horner family lived in a small house on the corner of Arthur Street and Franklin Street. The family was very large and it was rumored that Mrs. Horner was like the old woman that lived in a shoe. She had so many children, she didn't know what to do. At any rate there was an abundance of Horner kids, enough to form a gang. In our minds they were a major threat. During the spud wars, we joined forces with the equally large Farmer family. We were always afraid of being invaded by the Horner gang. We kept a separate stash of small potatoes to bean them if they ever attacked. Our snow forts had wings facing east, to protect us from the Horner gang. Icy snowballs were held in reserve. At Halloween you had to hold your bag tight and look over your shoulder in case one of the Horner gang grabbed it. We ad created a paper tiger. The Horner gang was not really a threat.

· · · · · · ·

I collected stamps for about ten years from ages eight to eighteen. In my younger years, I would use translucent hinges glued to the back of the stamp and then randomly mount the stamp on an album page for that country. I had a globe and a world atlas to help me identify the correct country and its location. It was a marvelous introduction to the subjects of geography and history.

As time went on, I learned to identify, catalogue and care for my stamps. You did not cut out stamps with scissors because it damaged the perforated edges; you did not soak or steam stamps to remove the envelope backing; you tried to keep the stamps in their original condition and you did not stick them in an album. You kept the stamps on special pages with slotted holes or in glassine envelopes and handled them carefully with tweezers.

My aunt, who worked at Canada Post in Ottawa, provided me with bags of Canadian stamps and my father collected stamps from all the international mail delivered to the Great Lakes Paper Company. My brother-in-law gave me his collection of stamps and I had many other sources that kept me supplied. When I was young, I sent away requests for stamps from the Majestic Stamp Company and the Empire Stamp Company. They would send stamps to me on approval. I would covet these stamps and buy as many as I could afford. These two companies kept me permanently supplied and broke. I would have to buy a postal money order at the downtown post office to pay for the stamps and then mail it to Toronto. Within two weeks, I would receive more stamps on approval and the cycle would be repeated It was addictive and I was hooked. I spent hundreds of hours of my young life working on my stamp collection. It certainly helped me to have a better understanding of the world that we live in. I have passed the collection on to my eldest son and trust that he or his sons may benefit from the collection.

. . . .

On Saturday mornings Jack Wren and I went to the YMCA for swimming lessons. Our parents wanted us to learn how to dive and swim. At the end of the one-hour lesson, the instructor would blow a whistle, signaling us to get out of the pool and head for the showers. I was always the last man out of the pool for a very good reason. We all swam naked in the pool and I usually had a "boner" or "hard-on" when we were summoned from the pool. These were slang names for a male penis erection.

The trouble was that the "boner" was unpredictable. You never knew when it was going to occur. It could be that it was when you were called up in front of the class to write something on the blackboard, forcing you to limp up the aisle with big lump in your pants. The girls would giggle and the boys would whisper "hard-on". It could also occur at the high school dance, when you were dancing with your current heartthrob, or even when you were singing a hymn in church, for heaven's sake.

I don't have the problem anymore.

· · · · · · ·

I was he only one in my male group of friends, who was not circumcised. When you are young, you don't want to be different. The fact that only an estimated one-third of males worldwide are circumcised was not comforting; nor was the fact that I was neither Jewish nor Islamic. I was still different.

Circumcision is the surgical removal of the foreskin from the human penis. It is usually removed for religious, cultural or health reasons. Medical organizations throughout the world do not recommend circumcision. Medically and statistically, I was on safe ground, but I still envied my friends who were circumcised. When I was at Isabella Public School, I would stand at the urinal checking out the size and shape of the neighboring penises.

I finally accepted my personal condition. My life has not been adversely affected. I did, however, have my sons circumcised, so that they would not have to experience my childhood trauma.

· · · · · · ·

It is very important to own a knife, particularly a Swiss Army knife with red handles and all sorts of accessories. The good ones had three knife blades, a corkscrew, a bottle cap opener, scissors, a nail file and a toothpick. I never owned a Swiss Army knife, but I wanted one badly. Knives were a symbol of manhood. Knife owners were respected. They were not used in our war games, but they were used for playing knife games, and making wooden walking sticks, whistles and guns.

The game of knife was played while sitting with your knife blade open and upright on your knee. You would then flip it off and if it landed and stuck upright in the ground, you won the game. You could also throw the knife while standing, to see if it would stick upright in the ground.

Both my mother and my wife did not approve of little boys owning knives, but I thought it was very important to own a knife, particularly a Swiss Army knife.

・・・・・・・

Before Grandma Dunn came to live with us, we always had one of the Galliant sisters living with us. They were from a large farming family in Hymers and employment as domestics was part of growing up. Certainly, there was nothing wrong with their work ethic. When one of the Galliant girls married or ran off, Mr. Galliant would merely send another as a replacement. The girls lived in and would do the housework, laundry, meal preparation and baby-sitting. They were never referred to as maids; I thought of them as being part of our family. They slept in the bedroom at the front of the house, helped serve our meals in the dining room and ate by themselves in the kitchen.

Lena was the first Galliant girl to work at our home. She was a really nice lady and looked after me as a preschooler. She would take my sister and me out to their farm on weekends and showed us how to ride a horse, milk a cow and have a squirt fight using the cow teat as a weapon. On Friday nights she would help us to make chocolate fudge, taffy and peanut brittle. We mixed up all the ingredients, cooked them on the stove and pulled the taffy until it was glossy and light in color. It was great fun. I was sorry when Lena left to marry a musician named Mike Bodnar. She was followed by a younger sister named Ella.

Ella was trouble. She liked the boys and sometimes was away overnight. Esje didn't approve and they had many disputes and altercations. Esje finally complained to Mr. Galliant and she was soon replaced by Dora.

Dora was the complete opposite, being rather meek and shy. She lasted until Grandma Dunn arrived to assume the household duties.

....

When I was eight years old, I received a ladle with an electric element for melting lead and a two-piece mold for creating lead soldiers. Esj would bring home bars of lead that were used for connecting the joints of plumbing pipe and would melt these into a liquid, skim of the scum and then pour the hot liquid lead into a hole at the top of the mold. The molds were prepared by blackening them with soot from a burning candle to keep the lead from sticking to the mold. The lead would then cool and solidify. I would then separate them molds, hoping that the finished casting was not missing an arm or a leg. There were a few war casualties. The injured soldiers would be returned to the ladle for melting.

If you wee lucky, all of your friends would own different molds allowing you to trade. Some soldiers were marching, some stood with rifles shouldered, some kneeled with rifles firing and some were on horses. Horses were hard to make.

I didn't know how he did it, but Roy Johnson always made better lead soldiers than me. I think that his father must of helped him. My father and mother had no idea what was going on in our basement and that I was busy poisoning myself with lead fumes. They did not recognize the danger of working with molten lead, an open candle flame, the constant danger of a spill and the toxic nature of lead exposure.

Humans have been mining and using lead for thousands of years. In my time lead was widely used in plumbing systems supplying dinking water, in the manufacture of metal food containers and in the manufacture of lead-based paint. We were touching lead, ingesting lead and breathing lead fumes. Lead poisoning was not recognized at the time. Years later it was found that lead interferes with a variety of body processes and is toxic to many organs and tissues including the heart, bones, intestines, kidneys, reproductive systems and nervous systems. It is particularly toxic to growing children.

JUST ME

Somehow, we all survived and to my knowledge none of my friends were affected.

· · · · · · ·

From age seven to ten, I was exposed to news about the Manchurian War, a dispute between Japan and China followed by the rise of the Third Reich and the war with Germany. During this time, I collected lead soldiers, which I had either made myself or had purchased from the local toy shop. I also bought army trucks, tanks, ambulances, anti-aircraft guns, howitzer cannons and aircraft. Of course, there was no use in collecting all of these war toys without having a war. It was staged in the spring, after the snow had melted and before our vegetable garden was planted. I had the ideal site to stage a war. With very little imagination, I could mound up the soil to make hills, valleys and roads. Trenches were constructed on either side of a zone called "no man's land." Mick Sutton and I then challenged two of our friends to fight a war. They brought in their troops and war equipment on Saturday, and we set up a war zone with their army on one side and our army on the other side. We were both armed with lead ammunition for our canons, and bombs for our aircraft. We then proceeded to destroy each other's fortifications.

I can't remember who won the war, but it was great fun.

· · · · · · ·

Big Little Books were first published in the 1930s and continued into the 1960s. The books were small and compact, typically 92 mm wide by 114 mm high and 38 mm thick. They originally sold for ten cents each. They had a hard cover and the contents of the book usually displayed full page black and white illustrations on the right side and text on the left. The stories were usually related to comic, cartoon and radio characters including Dick Tracy, Buck Rogers, Blondie, Mickey Mouse, Tarzan and dozens more. If you held a book in one hand and used your other hand to flip the pages, it was like watching a movie.

I was an avid collector of Big Little Books and exchanged them with my friends. The books are now collector's items selling for ten dollars each instead of ten cents and in any condition. I should have saved my collection of books.

• • • • • • •

I was always playing board games including Monopoly, Snakes and Ladders, Checkers and Bingo. I never learned to play Chess or Mahjong, which I regret. My favorite game was Monopoly. Monopoly is a board game that originated in the early 1900s and continues to this day. The current version was produced in the mid-1939s and I learned to play when I was about eight years old. My first game was played with my sister on a rainy summer day at our Amethyst camp. Each player begins with a roll of play money. In the game, players move a marker around the game board based on a throw of the dice, buying or trading properties that they land on, developing their properties with houses and hotels purchased with play money, and collecting rents from their opponents landing on their properties, with the goal being to drive your opponents into bankruptcy, leaving you in control of the economy. The games could last for hours and in the process, I learned about investment, risk taking and how our economy works. My kids play Monopoly, my grandchildren play Monopoly and I still like to play Monopoly.

• • • • • • •

I can't even remember what the initials TRC stand for except that they were pills that could cure every pain and disease imaginable. I'm sure that Grandma Dunn had some in her medicine drawer. Gilbert Templeton, not to be confused with Charles Templeton, the celebrated evangelist, author, radio and TV personality, would have a radio spot with a musical ditty. I remember it well:

Come round any old time, and make yourself at home,
Put your feet on the mantle shelf,

JUST ME

Open the cupboard and help yourself,
I don't care if your friends have left you all alone,
Rich or poor, just knock on the door and make yourself at home.

Then Gilbert would come on the air with his soothing and melodious voice saying: "Friends, if you have an upset stomach, lower back pain or aching joints, then try Templeton's TRCs for instant relief."

Gilbert's pills could cure anybody and anything. He was the reincarnation of the medicine man; in fact, he was the medicine man.

· · · · · · · ·

It is very important for a young boy to have a sandbox to play in. It is also very important for a cat to have a sandbox to poop in. Here are the seeds for a conflict. Esje had a sandbox built for me by one of the men at the mill. He was not handy with carpentry tools, but he was very good at delegating jobs to others. The sandbox was quite large. It was filled with a load of sand trucked from our cottage at Amethyst Harbor. I used to build roads, tunnels and bridges for my toy cars and trucks in the sand and I would also create battlegrounds for my guns and lead soldiers. The trouble was that Toots thought that my sandbox was just another big litter box that she could use when she went to the bathroom outside the house.
I was really angry one day, to discover that Toots had gone to the bathroom and had dug up an entire road system that I had just built in my sandbox. The roads led to the battlefront where I had all of my soldiers preparing for a war. She even knocked over some of my transport trucks and my sand observation tower.

The problem was that Toots had been trained to go to the toilet in a small box that was filled with sand. It was located in the basement beside her basket. She was very good about going to the bathroom. She would dig a small hole in the sand, sit over it and do her business and then cover it up. Cats do not do this because they are being polite, it is much more complicated. Cats are territorial. Toots territory was the front yard, the back yard and the house. Other cats were not welcome in this territory. Cats mark the boundaries of their territory by scratching or rubbing against things to leave their scent and also by leaving their feces uncovered. Feces and urine inside their territory are covered up. Toots thought that it was okay to go to the bathroom in a box filled with sand that was in her territory, as long as she covered it up. After all, a box is a box. Toots thought that it was okay to go to the bathroom in a box filled with sand. The trouble was that it was also my territory, and my toy army could not destroy a cat enemy. My father suggested that since this was a war, that I should stop fighting and sign a peace treaty with Toots and reach an agreement. I thought that this was a good idea and so, as part of the agreement, I made up a box that was the same size as the litter box in the basement and I filled it with sand from my sandbox. I put the small box in the backyard beside the big sand box. Then I printed out a peace treaty on a piece of paper, which said that I would use the large sandbox for building roads and playing with soldiers and that Toots would use her box to go to the bathroom. Each of us would then have our own territory.

I asked my best friend, Mick, to be a witness and I read the peace treaty to Toots. Then I pressed her paw into my black ink stamp pad and pressed her inky paw onto the peace treaty. It made a good print, but Toots didn't like it. She had to lick her paw for a long time to get rid of the ink.

Then I signed the peace treaty and Mick signed as a witness. From that day on, Toots used the small sand box, and I used the large box.

· · · · · · ·

I was always getting sick when I was growing up. If there was a communicable disease in Fort William. I contracted it. The last thing that you wanted was to become quarantined. In those days, there were no miracle drugs that we take for granted today. You had to contain the contagious disease t keep it from spreading throughout the community. If any member of our family contracted scarlet fever, mumps, chicken pox or measles, the local health officer would come around and attach a colored card on the front door, announcing to the world the nature of the disease and the fact that the house was quarantined and off limits. I didn't contract mumps until I was married and in my last year of university. Some claimed that mumps would affect my potency. Fortunately for my three children that did not occur.

Ear infections were frequent, and they would have to drain my ears with wicks to get rid of the gunk. Mustard plasters, consisting of a poultice of mustard seed spread inside a protective dressing were regularly applied to reduce congestion in my chest. I had my tonsils and adenoids removed, but my appendix behaved and is still with me. Dr. Wills, who was a good friend of the family, and lived close by, would regularly appear with his black bag, thermometer and stethoscope to check out my ears, throat and chest. He would usually gravely shake his head and announce that I was too sick to attend school. My joy in the announcement was not shared by my parents. Only the breadwinner could escape and go to work and he had to return to the house and not socialize. Depending on the disease, the quarantine would last from two to four week. It also depended on how many siblings you had and when they caught the disease. Large families were to be avoided.

All of my mother's friends agreed that I was a sickly child, including Mrs. Johnson. Every time I crossed her path, she would take a close look at me, shake her head and ask. "Are you not feeling well, Johnny? You don't look well." I avoided her. My parents decided that I should not take piano lessons, which I now regret, because I needed to be out in the fresh air. Somehow, I have survived and rarely get sick.

. . . .

There were no gasoline or diesel buses in my day. We had electric streetcars that served both Fort William and Port Arthur. Electricity was cheap, providing energy for transit, industry and municipal use. There were local generating stations at both Kakabeka Falls and Current River, operated independent of the Ontario power grid. The streetcars were connected to overhead wires with a spring-mounted pole that contacted the 600-volt overhead DC wire. The power was fed to direct current traction motors that were located on each wheel set. Braking was achieved by reversing the polarity of the power. Electric streetcars were a practical and economical solution for transportation and were eventually replaced by electric buses and subways. They were also an excellent way to flatten a penny when you put a penny on the rail.

. . . .

My first venture into retailing was with my two partners Mick Sutton and Sol Petroff. I was seven years old at the time, Mick was eight and Sol was six. Mick and I were sitting in my backyard one Saturday morning, wondering what to do.I suggested playing with our soldiers in the sandbox. Mick reminded me that we had done that the day before. He suggested playing badminton or setting up a game of croquet n the front lawn. I thought that it was too hot to play those games. We were quickly running out of ideas. Just then our neighbor Sol Petroff appeared. Mick and I asked him if he had any ideas and advised Sol that we had already eliminated soldiers, badminton and croquet. Sol thought for a few minutes and then suggested that we set up a store and sell something. Sol's father owned a shoe store and Sol said that his father knew all about selling stuff.

Mick asked what we should sell, but none of us had any ideas until Sol suggested that we could sell lemonade and that his mother would make it up for us. Mick then volunteered to get some beets and rhubarb from their garden.

Sol suggested that we could also sell some of our comic books and Big Little Books. I came up with the idea of selling empty wine bottles that we could collect from the neighbors, but Sol didn't like the idea and thought that wine bottles wouldn't sell. Mick cast the deciding vote and said that we should try it.

Then I had a great idea. Toots had just given birth to a new litter of kittens. They were about seven weeks old and could use the litter box. I thought that we could sell kittens.

Paul thought that it was a great idea, but Mick was not convinced and argued, that since we usually gave the kittens away for free, nobody would buy them. Paul suggested that we could advertise. He thought that there were plenty of new customers who would buy the kittens and we could sell them at fifty percent off. That was the way his father sold his shoes. We decided that the name of the store should be a combination of our surnames and ended up with the name Petsutour. Sol Petroff thought that it sounded like the name of a prehistoric dinosaur.

As retailers say, it's location, location, location. We located the store in my backyard for three very good reasons. The Suttons did not want it in their yard and the Petroff family felt the same way. I already had a shack in our backyard which could easily be converted into a store. When my mother was a young girl, her parents bought her an upright piano. It was a beautiful rosewood piano with ivory keys made by the Poole Piano Company. The manufacturer had packed the piano in a wooden box and shipped it from Boston, Massachusetts, to my mother's home in Keewatin, Ontario.

After my father and mother were married, they moved to Fort Frances and took the piano with them. During each move the piano was shipped in the original, wood packing box. When they decided to move to live permanently in Fort William, the box was not needed anymore. My father turned it into a playhouse for me, but I called it the shack.

The box was about two metres high by half a metre deep and made out of wood. The shack was constructed by turning the box upside down like a lid and raised above the ground and supported at each corner by four long wood posts with one end embedded in the ground. What had been the back of the piano box became the floor. Some empty wooden nail kegs served as chairs. It was like a small playhouse. The weathered words THIS SIDEUP were stenciled on the front of the box and the words POOLE PIANO COMPANY, with a directional arrow pointing to the front were imprinted on each side. A hand lettered cardboard sign that read Petsutour Store was tacked to the front edge of the box. Another sign reading KITTENS HALF PRICE, was tacked on the side.

We had collected some of our old toys and games for sale, while our mothers had provided cookies and lemonade. We had also gone around to our neighbor's garbage cans and salvaged some wine and liquor bottles to be sold at the store. There was a good supply of bottles at my neighbor's house. There were no bottles at the family that practiced Christian Science because of their belief in abstaining from drinking alcoholic beverages.

We hand lettered some signs on cardboard using chalk and then tacked them onto the piano box. Stocking the store was quite easy. Mick had permission to pull some rhubarb and beets from their garden; Sol's mother contributed a jug of lemonade and some paper cups; while I had no trouble convincing my parents to sell the kittens. Pricing was difficult. After some debate, we priced the bottles at one cent each, beets were four cents a bunch, books were two cents, the rhubarb was three cents a bunch, and lemonade was two cents a cup. The already discounted kittens were priced at ten cents each or fifteen cents for two.

By 10:30 Saturday morning the Petsutour was open for business. There were no customers. By 12:30 we had fourteen cents of our own money in the money jar after selling seven cups of lemonade. Most of the lemonade was now gone and the ice had melted. Sol went home to get some more lemonade and assured his mother that sales were brisk. He came back with a fresh jug and some matzo bread which had been left over from the Jewish Passover. We were starving. Mick went home and came back with some peanut butter and jelly sandwiches. I sneaked into our house and got a cup of sugar for dipping the unsold rhubarb. We sat around waiting for customers to appear and kept busy reading the Big Little Books and the comic books. Sol said that our poor sales were due to our poor location in the backyard and our lack of advertising. We were in the backyard and there was no traffic in the back lane. Sol suggested that we should be out front on the street advertising he store. We made up some new signs that Sol dreamed up. One said Liquidation Sale, which we thought tied in with the popularity of our lemonade.

Sales improved. One of the neighbors bought the beets, while another bought the remaining rhubarb. Sol went home for a third jug of lemonade. By 4:30 were all pretty tired of retailing and made up some new signs, which read Free Kittens and Free Bottles. There were still no sales.

Just as we were closing, Mr. Wills arrived home and visited the store. He did not recognize his recycled bottles under the counter and ordered two cups of lemonade half full. I thought that this was odd and then watched as he carried the cups into his garage, took a bottle marked paint thinner from the shelf, filled the cups and then drank them one after the other.

Sol was the only one of us that pursued a career in retailing, while Mick and I chose engineering. The kittens ended up on the Galliant farm to pursue a life of mousing.

JUST ME

· · · · · · ·

Like the story of Adam and Eve, Mrs. Petroff had commanded us not to eat her crab-apples, because she needed them to make crab-apple jelly. Nevertheless, she could not see what was going on behind the high wooden fence in her backyard. The crab-apple tree overhung the fence and was loaded with crab-apples. They ripened in late August, before we returned to school. As soon as it was dark, and before our evening bedtime call, we would take off on our bikes and head down the lane behind the Petroff house. We had to be very quiet because the Petroffs owned a dog that would bark loudly at the sight of its own shadow. If we leaned our bikes against the fence, you could stand on the crossbar, reach up, hold on to a branch, grab some crab-apples and stuff them in your shirt. At the same time, you had to watch out for Mrs. Petroff and the Horner gang. Loaded with crab-apples, we would ride back to the shack and feast on the forbidden fruit.

· · · · · · ·

My parents always encouraged me to have a job. They said that it builds character. My friend Roy Johnson and I both got jobs at the Central News Company, working for Henry Nash. Henry ran his company from a garage at the back of his property. He was a big man with a head to match, he was a formidable man. You couldn't fool Henry; he could account for every penny that you owed him. Roy and I delivered the *Star Weekly* and *Liberty* magazines. We each had to solicit our own customers and took advantage of family friends and neighbors. There was some overlap in our territories, but we were friendly competitors. Delivery in the spring, summer and fall was great, because we could use our bikes, but winter was another matter. We either had to carry our bags or use a sleigh. I also delivered the *Globe and Mail* for Mr. McCann. The newspaper was shipped from Toronto by train and arrived early in the morning a day later at the Canadian Pacific Railway station. I would pick up the papers for my route at six a.m. and deliver them before going to school. It was a tough job, but the pay was good at two cents per paper. With thirty papers on my route and a six-day week, I would gross $3.60 per week. The income financed the purchase of stamps for my collection. By the time I entered high-school, I found other ways to earn money. There were movies, records, and even dates with females to finance.

. . . .

We always spent our summer at our camp at Amethyst Harbor on Lake Superior. We initially lived on East Bay, then we moved to North Bay and ended up on South Bay. The harbor was originally used as a shipping port for amethyst from a nearby mine.

Amethyst is a purple or violet colored semi-precious gemstone that is found in various countries in the world. Some of the richest deposits were discovered hundreds of years ago near our camp at Amethyst Harbor.

There was an abandoned amethyst mine not far from our camp and as young boys we would hike over to the mine and search for leftover pieces of amethyst rock. We would walk along he CPR railway track to the mine and would spend our time shooting at the glass insulators on the hydro poles with stones from our slingshots. Fortunately, our aim was poor.

Amethyst is not as hard and not as clear or translucent as a precious gemstone. Precious stones include diamonds, rubies, emeralds and sapphires, while semi-precious stones include amethyst, quartz, agates and garnets. When Jack Stokes was Speaker of the Ontario Parliament, he adopted the practice of handing out small polished amethyst gemstones to visitors. It is the gemstone emblem for Ontario and was dear to his Northern Ontario heart. I am not sure who discovered amethyst in the Lake Superior area. It found in a granite fault or big crack which was formed billions of years ago. When they were first building the railway, someone found a piece of amethyst that was exposed near the surface of the crack, There is no record of who made the discovery but I do know that they mined amethyst years ago and shipped it from Amethyst Harbor.

The amethyst was mined by digging vertical shafts where the fault was located and then dynamite was used to extract large chunks of amethyst. These large pieces of stone were then shipped to various parts of the world for processing into smaller crystals and then into jewelry.

JUST ME

· · · · · · ·

We ate all our meals in the dining room. Our cat, Toots would always join us and sat on a corner chair, watching what we ate and supervising the meal. She always looked very dignified and never begged for food.

Cats are not like dogs. Despite thousands of years of living with humans, they are still carnivores. They cannot survive without eating meat. That is why they catch and eat mice and birds. A cat eats just like a lion or a tiger. They don't eat plants. A dog, on the other hand, is just like us. It will eat anything, whether it is plant or animal.

Cats are also very fussy about when to eat. They like to eat a small amount of food twice a day, usually in the morning and afternoon. I think that we would all be better off if we ate like cats. Fat cats are rare. There was some commercial cat food on the market in the 1930s. Usually it was wet food made from low-cost fish and meat which could not be sold to the public. We used to buy Spratts cat food. Dried food, like kibble was not available. Most of the food that Toots ate was leftover meat and poultry that my grandmother ground up so that she would not choke on the bones. Toots really loved liver and fish. We usually had liver once a week and we always had fish on Friday.

· · · · · · ·

As a six-year-old, I can remember in the morning, seeing men sitting on our back steps waiting for a handout. These were hard times, the Depression years. The men were called hobos and did not have jobs. They rode the rods. There are steel tension rods that formed a truss supporting the platform of a box car. The men would lie on the rods only a short distance from the fast-passing rail bed. Hobos did not go to sleep when they rode the rails. The hobos hitched rides on freight trains that travelled across Canada. The moved from one place to another looking for work. They wanted jobs very badly and travelled anywhere looking for work. These men were not like "tramps", who worked only when they were forced to, and they were not like 'bums', who did not work at all.

These were *The Great Depression* years. Millions of people were without work all over the world. That period of time was also called *The Dirty Thirties*. Few countries were affected as severely as Canada. There was no market for our grain, wood and minerals. The Prairie Provinces suffered the most. My wife Pat and her family lived on a farm near Prince Albert, Saskatchewan. There was no market for wheat, and the farms were also affected by drought, plagues of grasshoppers and hailstorms. Most of the farmers went bankrupt and lost their homes. Some of the younger people decided to "ride the rods", looking for work. There were job opportunities in the provinces of Ontario and Quebec, so men from the Prairies hitched rides on the freight trains carrying grain to eastern Canada. These were the men who were sitting on our backsteps. Hobos were good men and usually young men. You had to be young enough and agile enough to jump on to a moving train and then lay on the rods, inches from the passing rail. Many died in the attempt and were crushed under the wheels. These men were just down on their luck. My grandmother would feed them with a bowl of porridge, warm milk and brown sugar. After the men finished their porridge, grandma would bring out some tea and stale bread with lard spread on the top. Some of the men had lost most of their teeth and would dip the bread in their tea to soften it up. Stale bread with lard is actually quite nourishing. There are a lot of good vitamins and minerals in it. I don't think that my grandmother knew anything about nutrition. She just knew that she had lard on toast as a young girl and it was cheaper and better than eating a piece of stale bread all by itself.

Once the men had finished their meal, they would volunteer to do some chores around the house. My grandmother kept a list of "things to do", which included cutting the grass, weeding the garden, taking out the garbage and picking raspberries. The work was fair payment for a good breakfast. The hobos just wanted a "hand up" and not a "handout". It was interesting how the hobos found our house. They had developed a system of symbol or a sign code using chalk or coal to draw a sign A picture of two connected rings depicted handcuffs meaning police are here. There was a train track close to our home and the trains would slow down when they were in the city. There were telephone and electrical poles erected beside the track and the hobos would attach their signs to the poles. On a pole close to our home, they had posted a sign with a cat on it and the numerals 1416 underneath. The sign meant that you could get food from a kind old lady who owned a cat and lived in a house whose number was 1416. The sign worked, because there were always three or four men at our back door every day. Toots was always there to greet them and get a backrub and a bit of leftover milk and porridge.

． ． ． ． ． ． ．

The Beaman family lived up the lane. Their cat was the mother of our cat. According to my sister, she brought Toots home and claims that Toots was her cat. I disagreed and always claimed that Toots was our cat. Toots made her home in a wicker baby carriage basket located in the basement. Toots played an important part in my young life and I wrote a novel about her, titled *The Keyhole - The Adventures of Toots the Cat*. I dedicated the novel to my sister. Toots was very popular with the male cats in the neighborhood and regularly produced two litters of kittens per year.

I remember on one occasion she had a litter of five instead of the usual four. One of them could never find a nipple for feeding and since kittens must take milk in the first twenty-four hours, it starved to death. I put the dead kitten in a small cardboard box and buried it out in the garden. I made a cross, using two popsicle sticks, and stuck the cross in the ground to mark the grave Being unfamiliar with feline eulogies, I bowed my head and prayed, "Goodbye, good luck, and good hunting." I christened the remaining four kittens, Eeny, Meeny, Miny and Moe like the counting-out rhyme. Toots had many more kittens during her lifetime and some of them died after birth There were many more crosses in the garden graveyard.

Toots introduced me to the birth experience, the rearing of new-born, and the death experience. When kittens are first born, they are attached to the mother with an umbilical cord. This is used for feeding the kittens when they were in Toot's womb. The first thing that Toots did when each kitten arrived was to nip through the umbilical cord with her teeth. Then she would lick each kitten clean which helped the kittens to breathe properly. In the beginning, Toots spent most of her time nursing. She would only leave the kittens to go to her litter box or to feed herself. The kittens did not all nurse at the same time and sometimes they would fall asleep on the job. Toots spent a great deal of her time licking the kittens and keeping them clean. I always kept some old newspapers in the bottom of the basket and changed them daily. At the end of three weeks, Toots would leave the kittens for short periods of time so that she could clean herself and use the litter box. If one of the kittens should start to cry, she would immediately go back and take care of it. If the kitten wandered away from the basket, she would pick it up by the furry scruff of the neck and return it to the basket. This did not hurt the kitten, because she was not biting into the skin.

Kittens are not able to see, when they are first born. Their eyes are closed, and their ears are folded down. By the end of two weeks their ears have begun to straighten out and their eyes are fully open. The kittens now have all five senses: sight, hearing, taste, smell and touch. The eyes of all kittens are blue at first and do not change to their adult color for many months. During the third and fourth weeks, the kittens tried to stand up. Their legs were quite shaky, and they attempted to follow Toots whenever she left the basket. She fed them very little and at that time I started giving them some adult food using a teaspoon. At first, I mixed up evaporated milk and water plus a little bit of baby cereal. Then after a few more weeks, I added some chopped-up fish and gave them some water. Kittens do not need a large amount of food to survive.

Toilet training began after about five weeks. Toots taught by example. Kittens are very good at imitating their mother. The kittens would follow Toots over to the litterbox and she would dig a small hole on the sand to do her business. Then she would cover it up. The kittens would then imitate what she had done. The completion of toilet training also meant that the time had come for the kittens to leave our home.

Most of our neighbors and friends already owned cats and dogs. They didn't want any kittens. Our maid Lena came to the rescue. She came from a farm where cats were always welcome. Toots' kittens became barnyard cats and ere kept busy in the ongoing farm battle with rats and mice. Toots had already taught her children about the rudiments of hunting by presenting them with a dead mouse. They very quickly learned to be good barnyard cats, because that was to be their only source of food.

During the entire kitten rearing period, the tomcat or father of the kittens never appeared. Animals, birds and insects all have different rules for raising their children. In the cat family, the rule is that the female cat is the mother, and she looks after the kittens. The tomcat or daddy can stay away, because he does not like other male cats in his territory and that includes male kittens. That rule applies to all cats, including lions and tigers.

• • • • • • •

There was a swimming hole on the Neebing River, just behind the tuberculosis hospital. We could easily ride there on our bicycles and on a hot summer day, when it was too warm to play games, we would go the for a swim. Our parents knew that we went swimming at the river, and they said it was okay as long as the river was not flooding due to high runoff. The Neebing River meandered through our city and eventually joined up with another river called the McIntyre, before emptying into Lake Superior. It did not usually carry much water and flowed slowly. The river was considered to be safe. If there had been a heavy rainstorm, however, the water would rise and flood rapidly, overtopping its banks, and creating a dangerous condition.

We skinny-dipped or went bare balls in a swimming hole located at a deep spot on the river. There was a limb from an adjacent willow tree that hung down over the hole. We tied a rope to the limb of the tree so that we could hold on with both hands and swing through the air like Tarzan. Then we let go of the rope and cannonballed into the water. A good cannonball was achieved by tucking your body into a ball, and using your arms, pulling your knees up to your chest and holding them there. Then you closed your eyes, held your breath and let go. I was able to make a really great splash. The character Tarzan appeared in a Walt Disney movie series called Tarzan of the Apes and was very popular. Tarzan was a young orphan boy who was raised by a family of apes in the jungle. He learned how to swing through the air by hanging on to tree vines.

• • • • • • •

I think that the phrase *Thank You* is one of the most important phrases in the English language. The one phrase that we all remember rom our high school French lesson is *Merci Beaucoup* meaning *Thank You*. I am impressed when children, trick or treating on Halloween say *thank you* for their treats or you receive a *thank you* response when you compliment someone on their good work or their appearance. My cat Toots had a most unusual way of saying *thank you*. She would say thanks by depositing a dead mouse in my shoe. It was Toots way of saying *thank you* to me for providing her with a good home and food. She was very proud when she caught a mouse and for her, a mouse was a valuable possession. She was giving me the dead mouse because she appreciated her home and food and wanted to say thank you. I am constantly thanking people for helping me with my current walking disability. They hold doors open, pick up unreachable objects, pour drinks, fill plates and help me dress. I could not function without their help. Thank you!

Historically, Christians ate fish on Friday, because every Friday was a fast day, and fish counted as poor people's food. In the secular world *fasting* means going on a disciplined diet. The purpose of the fast is to find out who is in control; you or your stomach and to win that control if necessary. It's a religious snooze alarm. When I was growing up, we always had fish on Friday. It was usually lake trout or pickerel. I looked forward to eating fish. I love eating fish. Nowadays we have fish quite often on any day of the week. I particularly like salmon with lemon and my wife cooks a wicked sole in egg batter with breadcrumbs.

· · · · · · ·

Our camp or should I say cottage was located on the North Bay of Amethyst Harbor. It was quite large, two stories high. There were three bedrooms downstairs and the upstairs was just one big open room. That is where I slept. The cottage was uninsulated and since it was a summer residence, there had not been a great deal of care in closing all the cracks and crevices in the outside walls. In short, there were plenty of places where a bat could squeeze through the wall for a nice warm and dry nesting place. Unknown to us, they did it frequently. Bats are not attention seekers and they arrived, nested and departed silently. The only traces they left were some droppings. My grandmother constantly complained that we had mice upstairs, since their droppings are identical to those of a bat. I knew better.

Occasionally a bat would become confused and find itself flying around in my second-floor bedroom with no way to get out. I was usually able to catch it with a fish net. I found a fish net useful because a bat will fly around and then land high up on a vertical surface, like a curtain or drape. Usually, I opened up all the windows for the bat to escape, but this allowed more than our quota of mosquitoes to enter. The net worked best with the windows closed.

Bats are very beneficial. We had plenty of mosquitoes at the cottage and one bat can catch from 500 to 1000 mosquitoes per hour. Bats use echoes to catch the mosquito. They produce a very high-pitched sound that we cannot hear and then wait for it to hit a small object, like a mosquito. The sound will echo back to their sensitive ears. They can then calculate where the mosquito is located and catch it. The marvelous thing is, that they can do all this in a fraction of a second and then keep repeating it. Our modern-day radar works the same way and is modelled after a bat.

We had a bat nesting box on a laundry pole in our backyard. It was quite high and had a slit at the bottom for bats to enter. It was facing south, so that it would be exposed to the sun most of the day. The bats liked a warm nest, and the box was well used.

· · · · · · ·

There was a park, at the end of Cuthbertson Place. It was called Vickers Park. At the far edge of the park, there was a large, flat open field. Many years ago, an ambitious land developer had surveyed the area and then laid out a patchwork grid of streets, which were identified by ditches dug into the ground. The streets had never been constructed and there were no houses. As time passed, willow bushes had grown up in the ditches. The ditches and open fields provided us with a great place to play and we spent many happy hours on the other side of the park.

The ditches and willow bush provided us with an ideal location to build a secret hideout, where we would get together and have meetings. We couldn't use the ditches in the spring, because they were quite wet, but for most of the summer, the ditches were dry. We built a hideout at the end of one of the ditches near the park. As the only boy in our family, I had always wanted to have a brother, preferably an older brother. My three best friends all had older brothers and I thought it would be great to have someone close, who I could communicate with; someone with whom I could share both my secrets and my worries; someone who would help me with my homework; someone who would show me what to do next. I loved to read. There were no television or electronic games to distract a young boy in the 1930s. Our local library was my refuge and my pleasure. It opened up an exciting new world for me. I had read most of the young adult adventure books that were available and also any books that dealt with Canadian history. One of the stories that I read described a blood brother ritual, where males would mix their blood, bringing them together into a family. They also pledged loyalty to each other. I thought this was a great idea, particularly since I didn't have a brother of my own. I suggested to my best friend Mick and my second-best friends Roy and Art that we could become blood brothers. They all liked the idea. We decided to have a blood brother ceremony at our hideout. I borrowed four needles from my grandmother's sewing basket and a small plate from the kitchen. Mick brought some matches and a candle. We all met at the hideout after church on a Sunday afternoon.

I lit the candle and gave each of my friends a needle. You have to heat the needle until it is red hot to sterilize it. I had read that dirty needles spread disease. Then you prick the end of your finger and put a drop of your blood in the middle of the plate. My friend Mick was not sure that we should be doing this on Sunday, but Roy, the scholar, advised him that the Bible says that you should not eat or drink blood, but there is nothing mentioned about mixing blood to become brothers. I reminded the others that a blood brother is a male who swears loyalty to, another male.

Each of us added a few drops of blood to the plate. Then I mixed the blood together with my forefinger and then made a mark on the forehead of Mick, Roy and Art. I finished up by marking my own forehead with blood. Then I consulted my notes and asked my blood brother to repeat an oath of loyalty. We spoke in unison.

"My brothers we have mixed and shared our blood. Each of us now bears the mark of that sharing. We promise that we shall be loyal to each other at all times; that we shall help each other, when help is needed; and we shall share as brothers both fortune and misfortune. Amen."

Everyone agreed that it was a pretty good oath. I never told them that I had made it up. Mick, Roy and Art remained friends for life – true blood brothers.

· · · · · · · ·

My cat Toots had a problem. She was afraid of dogs and would run away if she saw a dog. The dog, of course would chase her. Dogs will chase after any animal that runs away from them, because that is the way that dogs think and that is the way dogs act. If Toots had just stood in front of the dog and hissed, then the dog would not have chased her. The dog might even have decided to like Toots, and become friends, but Toots always chose to run when she saw a dog and that could lead to big trouble. Toots could actually run faster than the dog, and she would run to the closest tree and climb up to escape. Dogs, of course cannot climb trees.

We had a big old silver birch tree in our front yard, and it was higher than the house. It was the highest tree on the street. It was a beautiful tree and had been planted long before our house was built. Birch trees are very versatile. Our Canadian Indians used to cut bark from birch trees for the construction of canoes. Birchwood is also hard and can be fashioned into attractive furniture. We always burned birchwood in our fireplace. The bark was easy to ignite, and the logs burned for a long time. Part of our birch tree had rotted where a branch had been cut off. My father and I dug out the rotten wood and filled the hole with concrete. As the years passed, the wound in the tree healed itself and hid our cosmetic surgery. I can imagine that some future woodcutter would be quite surprised when his chainsaw hit the concrete.

The birch tree was also good for climbing, because there was one big branch that was just my height, and I could grab hold of it with both hands and then hoist myself up. Then I would climb higher so that I could look over the roof of our house. I never climbed to the top of the tree, because the branches were small and started to bend under my weight.

One day Toots was chased by our neighbor's dog. She ran and climbed the birch tree in our front yard. The dog stood at the base of the tree and barked loudly. The more the dog barked, the higher Toots climbed, until she was higher than she had ever climbed before. She was even higher than I had climbed, and the branches bent down under her weight. Toots was frightened and started to mew. She did not know how to get down. The dog eventually got tired of barking and went home. Toots was making quite a fuss and mewing loudly by this time. A neighbor called me to see if I could coax Toots down from the tree. I got a dish of her favorite cat food from the house and put it at the base of the tree. Toots loved the cat food, and I was sure that she would come down to get it. The problem was that Toots had climbed up so high, that she could not turn around and she did not know how to come down backwards. That was the way that I came down. By this time, a large group of neighbors had gathered around the birch tree and they were offering suggestions on how to get Toots down from the tree. Someone suggested using a long pole with a fish net on the end, but there was not a pole that was long enough. Another suggested an extension ladder, but there were so many branches on he birch tree that you could not get close to Toots. Another suggested that we should just leave the cat alone and it would eventually figure out a way to get down. I decided to take matters into my own hands. I climbed up the tree to make the rescue, just like my hero, Tarzan.

I had never climbed that high before, but there was always a first time. When I got close to Toots, the tree branches started to bend quite badly. The minute Toots saw me, she jumped and landed on my shoulder. The tree branch that was supporting me, bent down further with our combined weight and my foot got wedged into an adjoining branch. I was trapped. I could not get my foot out and I shouted for help. Now both Toots and I needed rescuing. My father, in the meantime, had arrived and took charge. He ordered my mom to phone the fire department for help and also to phone the animal control officer to come and get rid of Toots once and for all.

It only took a few minutes. A fire truck with big extension ladders arrived. They unloaded one of the ladders and leaned it against the tree. One of the firemen climbed the ladder and after cutting away a few branches, he was able to reach in and rescue both Toots and me. The crowd at the base of the tree all cheered. My dad was really mad at me for causing all this trouble. I was in tears. Toots, in the meantime was finishing off the cat food at the base of the tree. The animal control officer arrived and when Toots saw him with his bag, she ran back to the house and hid in her basket down in the basement. My father insisted that Toots must go. The fire department had been called unnecessarily. She was always causing trouble and he was sick of it. I pleaded with him not to send Toots away, but he would not change his mind. The animal control officer found Toots in her basket, put her in his bag and took her away. The only good thing was that Toots gave the animal control officer a good scratch that actually drew blood.

A month later, Toots appeared sitting on the kitchen windowsill. Somehow, she had found her way home. The animal control officer swore on a stack of Bibles that he had taken Toots eleven km away to Kakabeka Falls, and that she must have made her way home on her own. My father never said another word about Toots leaving home. She was safe forever.

· · · · · · ·

Mick and I spent the summer together at our Amethyst Harbor cottage. The cottage was located on North Bay. There was a creek that flowed between our property and the neighbor's property. Some of the old timers in the area called it Beaver Creek, but we didn't know why. The creek provided Mick and I with an endless source of entertainment. We could build a dam and create a small pond where the creek entered the bay; we could catch tad poles and keep them in the pond; we could have boat races; and we even fished unsuccessfully for brook trout in the pond.

The tadpoles or polliwogs are baby frogs that swim around in the water. They have a large, flattened tail that allows them to wiggle or swim. They have no arms or legs. As they grow older, the legs start to develop followed by the arms. Then the tail becomes shorter, the eyes get larger and the small mouth at the front of the head grows wider. The little frog then begins to breathe air and emerge from the water. It is really quite wonderful how different animals evolve. Mick and I used to have races with the baby frogs. We would draw a circle in the sand and then we would each put a frog in the middle of the circle. The first frog to hop out of the circle won the race. Sometimes we would get our frogs mixed up because they all look alike. We also had to keep Toots away from our game, because she liked to chase and catch frogs.

One day, Mick and I decided that we would explore the source of the creek and find out where it began. It was morning, so we packed a lunch of peanut butter and jelly sandwiches and a couple of bottles of pop. There was no canned pop in those days. It all came in bottles. Mick decided to take along a compass so that we would not get lost. The compass was to become a big source of disagreement between Mick and me.

We packed our knapsacks and started off on the exploration trip. There was a fisherman's path on one side of the creek, which made the first part of our trip pretty easy. But soon the creek became smaller and shallower with no pools for the brook trout. The path disappeared and only an animal track remained. Mick and I made our way upstream for several kilometers and eventually found a beaver dam. This explained why the locals called the stream Beaver Creek.

The creek then emerged into an area clear of small trees and brush, with only a few large birch and poplar trees remaining. A forest of small stumps with neatly chewed spear-like ends guarded the pond. The beavers had been at work harvesting the trees to create the dam. The dam stretched in an arc around more than half the perimeter of the pond. There was a pile of branches and twigs, all covered in mud near the edge of the pond. It was the beaver's home, a lodge. There was no entrance visible. It was underwater so that no intruder could get in. Mick and I scanned the pond looking for telltale ripples or the exposed head of the beaver. There was nothing visible. Beavers are nocturnal animals that work at night and sleep by day. We sat down at the edge of the dam. Opened our knapsack and ate our lunch. With no beavers in sight and the source of the creek discovered, Mick and I decided to head back to the cottage. Rather than returning by way of the creek, we decided to head for a road to the cottage. It was called the North Bay Road. After a discussion we decided that since we had come from North Bay that we would use Mick's compass to find our way home. The trouble was that Micks older brother had given him the compass and had not explained how to use it. We decided that since the compass needle always pointed north, then all we had to do was to walk in that direction and we would reach the North Bay Road. We started out quite confident; the compass reading weas quite simple and we would be home in time for supper. An hour later we were not sure and two hours later we knew that we were lost. I was an avid reader and collector of Hardy Boy books. In one story, Frank Hardy was lost and found his way home by checking the growth of moss on trees According to the story, since the sun shines on the south side of the tree, the moss will grow on the shaded or north side of the tree. The problem was that there were so many trees, that there was no sun, and the moss grew on all sides of the tree. Finally, we found an open area and there was some moss on only one side of several trees. I assured Mick that now we knew which way was north, we could find our way home. Mick, in the meantime was shaking his head. His compass had merely confirmed my tree theory. We were still lost. We should have just followed the creek back. We eventually did find the creek and followed it back home. . . The piano has played a very important part in the history of our family. Our piano was an upright Poole piano, manufactured in Boston, Massachusetts. My mother was given the piano when she was in her teens and it has travelled with our family ever since. It is a beautiful piano made of rosewood with ivory-capped keys. My mother gave the piano to me and I gave the piano to my daughter Colleen. The piano is now more than one hundred years old, and I hope that it remains in the family. When I was growing up, the piano played a very big part in family life. There was no television, and radio was in its infancy. We entertained ourselves by playing and singing songs around the piano. Both my mother and my sister played, so there was no shortage of pianists. We loved music. I never learned to play, but I do love to sing and joined in the Collingwood Sound Investment Choir after I retired. Years later, I wrote a novel titled Songs Old and New. It became a Bestseller.

. . . .

THOMAS MCCAVOUR

Music from the 1930s was generally upbeat and sometimes very relaxing. Humor was an important element in popular music. Swing ad jazz dominated the music scene and musicals were also quite popular. Some of the well-loved songs included:

Begin the Beguine by Cole Porter;
But Not For Me by the Gershwin Brothers;
Cheek to Cheek by Irving Berlin;
Easter Parade by Irving Berlin;
I've Got You Under My Skin by Cole Porter;
My Funny Valentine by Rodgers and Hart;
Night and Day by Cole Porter;
Smoke Gets in Your Eyes by Jerome Kern;
The Song Is You by Jerome Kern

My favorite 1930s song was Easter Parade:

In your Easter bonnet
With all the frills upon it
You'll be the grandest lady
In the Easter parade

I'll be all in clover
And when they look you over
I'll be the proudest fellow
In the Easter parade

On the avenue, Fifth Avenue
The photographers will snap us
And you'll find that you're
In the rotogravure

I would write a sonnet
About your Easter bonnet

JUST ME

And of the girl I'm taking
To the Easter parade

On the avenue, Fifth Avenue
The photographers will snap us
And you'll find that you're
In the rotogravure

. . . .

There were some great songs in the 1940s. The top songs from the movies included:

Over The Rainbow from The Wizard of Oz
As Time Goes by from Casablanca in 1942;
White Christmas from Holiday Inn in 1942;
When You Wish Upon a Star from Pinocchio in 1940;
I'll Never Smile Again by Tommy Dorsey in 1940;
Only Forever by Bing Crosby in 1940;
Frenesi by Artie Shaw in 1940;
Song of the Volga Boatmen by Glenn Miller in 1941;

My favorite was White Christmas;

(Christmas, white Christmas)
I'm dreaming of a white Christmas
Just like the ones I used to know
Where the treetops glisten
And children listen
To hear sleighbells in the snow

I am dreaming of a white Christmas
With every Christmas card I write
May your days be merry and bright
And may all your Christmasses be white

(I'm dreaming of a white Christmas)
(With every Christmas card I write)
May your days be merry and bright
And may all your Christmasses be white

· · · · · · · ·

I always enjoyed watching the kittens play with each other and when they grew older, I enjoyed playing with them. Most mammals play when they are youngsters, and some continue even when they are grown up. Even birds play, but I have never known fish or cold-blooded frogs or snakes to play. The most playful species are dolphins, apes, monkeys and most carnivores.

Kittens learn by playing. It teaches them how to get along with each other, how to survive, how to hunt and how to keep physically fit. I often think that we as human beings would be much better off if we spent more time playing during our childhood.

It takes about three weeks before a kitten is interested in playing. By that time, they can see and are not busy feeding. It is mostly rough and tumble-play. By the fourth week, they have learned how to wrestle with each other, clasping with their front paws and kicking with their rear legs. By the fifth week, they have learned to pounce on each other. This is a skill that will be used in their adult life to catch mice. Swatting and scooping come next in preparation for hunting birds and fish. It is usually these traits that are used when cats play with humans.

They will mouse-pounce on a trailing piece of string or the twitching end of Toots' tail. They will bird swat at a dangling piece of ribbon and fish-scoop a rolling ball of string. It is all about learning and practicing by playing.

As the kittens grow older there is less play and by the time they become adults, playing is rare. The love of play is never completely lost. Even old cats can be encouraged to chase a rolling ball or swat an imaginary bird. I always felt sorry for kittens that grow up alone and do not have the stimulation of playing with brothers and sisters.

Toots provided us with an endless supply of kittens, and we had continuous entertainment.

JUST ME

. . . .

It was a warm weekend in spring. The snow had disappeared from the fields with the long brown grass from the previous year pressed close to the ground. The soil was still soggy from the winter melt, but the grass was dry. My blood brothers and I were having a meeting at our hideout in the ditch. The ditch was a little wet, so we decided to dry things out with a fire. We had trouble starting the fire because the twigs and kindling were still wet from the winter snow. Some birch bark, peeled from one of the trees in the park, solved the problem. I have no idea how the grass fire started, but it was windy, and a random spark must have ignited some grass close to our hideout. Grass fires are tricky. They can smolder and go unnoticed. With a little wind, the fire will flare up and spread very quickly, producing a great deal of smoke. We had some sacks in our hideout that we could use to beat out the flames. With four of us working, we thought the fire was under control, but it sprang up in three more locations, ignited by airborne hot ash. The wind was our enemy. The fire was out of control. We could hear the fire trucks coming. Someone had seen the smoke and alerted the fire department. We decided to flee the scene. We watched what was going on from the park. The fire trucks arrived, but there were no fire hydrants to supply water The fields were still too wet to support the weight of the pumper truck. It would have got stuck. The firemen had to backpack twenty-three kg water cannisters over uneven ground to chase the fire. The ditches did not stop the rampage. The wind merely carried the hot embers to the neighboring fields. It took several hours to get the fire under control.

While we were sitting in the park watching the firemen at work, a police officer approached us. He said that there were reports of some small boys playing in the fields before the fire started. He then asked if we were the boys and if we had started the fire. We all looked at each other and remembered our blood brother oath. We did not tell lies, but we stuck together. I stood up for the group and admitted that it was us. The police officer announced that he could take us all down to the police station and charge us with arson. It was very expensive to have the fire department out fighting a grass fire. We could be fined for the cost involved. I pleaded that the fire had not been deliberate and that when it started, we had tried our best to put it out. The wind had made that impossible. The police officer relented and left us with a warning that if this ever happened again, we would all go to jail.

. . . .

We always cut our own tree a few days before Christmas. It was usually a spruce tree. There was a conservation area within the city limits that allowed Fort William residents to cut trees. It was out on the islands at the mouth of the Kam River and was only a twenty-minute drive from our house. The trees that you could cut were all tagged. But the nice thing was that they were free. My father would load up the car with an axe, a small swede saw, and some rope to tie the tree down to the roof of the car. We arrived at the site and then headed into the bush to find the perfect tree. That was always a problem because each of us had a different idea about perfection. My mother liked short and bushy, my sister liked tall and slim, while I liked a bushy bottom and a nice taper to a medium height. My father said that he didn't care . . . Just get on with it. Eventually, with a little bit of compromising, we settled on a tree that satisfied most of our specifications. The tree was duly chopped down, and we were quite surprised at its size. When you are outdoors trees appear to be smaller than they really are. The tree was obviously too big, so we made the first amputation with the swede saw and cut off about thirty cm. Then we dragged the tree out to the car and when my father, who had not been with us during the initial selection and harvesting, announced that the tree was much too big to carry on the roof of the car. A second amputation with the swede saw reduced the length of the tree by another thirty cm. We tied the tree to the roof of car and headed home. We arrived home with our trophy tree and were quite surprised when my grandmother came out of the house; took one look and announced that it would never fit inside the house. It was not only too high, but it was too bushy. So, we removed an additional thirty cm from the tree and pruned back the lower branches, which originally had been a compromise to satisfy mother's bushy condition. A wood base shaped like a cross was then nailed to the end of the tree and we carried our amputee patient indoors. When we tilted the tree upright, it was discovered that the top leader of the fir tree bent over when it hit the ceiling. So, we then cut off another ten cm to make it fit. We also pruned back some more of the lower branches that were hitting an adjacent armchair. The tree was now thinner and one metre shorter.

Since the tree was not perfectly straight, we put a wedge under one side of the wood base, so that it appeared to be upright. My mother had all of the decorations from the previous year ready. They had been packed away in boxes and stored in the basement. We started to decorate.

The first job was to get the lights to work. These were old strings, and if one light burned out, then all of the remaining lights on the string went out. My dad was in charge of the lights and after much cursing and prayers to whichever god was in charge of lighting, he got the first string to work. The second and third strings were easier, and the cursing was not as loud or as frequent. Fortunately, Grandma was slightly deaf and did not hear my father. She read her Bible every night and definitely did not approve of swearing. My father's remarkable vocabulary was not acceptable to her.

After the lights were strung, we applied tinsel, made from aluminized paper to simulate icicles hanging from a tree. Toots always sat and watched the decorating. She liked tinsel. She could bat it with her paw. The glass balls went on next. From experience gained from past ball attacks and breakage, we put them high enough so that Toots could not reach them. A few strings of popcorn were added, and the tree was finished. At least we thought it was finished until my mother removed the wrapper from the forgotten Star of Bethlehem. Since the star had to go on the top of the tree, another ten cm had to be lopped off. The total amputations from the original cutting was now more than a metre. Of course, we could have taken along a measuring tape, when we originally cut the tree down, but that's hindsight. We were all sitting back admiring our handiwork, when my sister appeared with two turtle doves. They had feathers and were quite realistic, representing the two turtle doves in a Christmas Carol. She had saved and bought them with her own money. I suggested that she could have saved money by buying just one partridge. She just ignored me and hung the birds in a prominent spot near the top of the tree. Toots had been sitting by, watching the decorating and she was very interested in the doves. The birds looked quite real to her, except they didn't move, and they didn't make a sound. We finished off the day with a glass of mulled cider to celebrate our tree decorating project and then hung up our socks for Santa's arrival. Toots just kept watching the doves and secretly planned her next move. We all retired for the night, pleased with our creativity and looked forward to the Christmas Day ahead. Toots did not retire. She wanted to catch those doves. When it was dark, she crept from her basket in the basement and went upstairs. Cats cannot see when it is completely dark, but when there is a little light, they can see quite well. The hall light beside the living room was on. Toots could see quite clearly. The doves were still on the Christmas tree, silent and motionless. Toots crept slowly with her belly close to the carpet in her best hunting form. She jumped onto the forbidden sofa and then jumped again onto the tree and grabbed one of the doves. The Christmas tree came crashing down and Toots ran off with the dove. The house was silent.

The next morning, I was the first one up, discovered the mess and started to clean it up. We all thought that the tree had fallen over on its own. My dad blamed it on the wedge that we had used. Later on, I found the dove in my boot. It was a gift. I guess that it was Toots' way of saying Merry Christmas! It was our secret, and I never told the family, that Toots made the tee fall when she jumped and grabbed the dove.

· · · · · · ·

My ancestors came from Kilkeel, Ireland in the 1800s and settled in Lorneville, New Brunswick. They earned their living fishing for cod and salmon in the Bay of Fundy. Lobsters that were pulled up in their nets were usually thrown back into the ocean. Some were taken home and they were cooked, but they were considered to be a poor man's food. At school, one peanut butter and jelly sandwich was a fair trade for two lobster sandwiches.

As time passed, the cod were fished out and the fishermen decided to harvest lobster using wooden traps, baited with fish and with openings that allowed the lobster to enter but not escape. Lobster was originally only eaten by people who lived by the sea, but as it became more popular, it was refrigerated using ice and was shipped to nearby locations by train.

There was a fish store in New Brunswick, owned by one of my cousins and he would pack the live lobster in wooden barrels filled with ice and seaweed. Then he would ship the barrels by train to our home in Fort William. It took about four days to get there. When the barrel arrived, my father would pick them up, take them home and then unpack them, hoping the lobsters were still alive. The only place that he could think of putting the lobsters was the laundry tub in the basement. He didn't tell my mother. She would have been horrified, but since she never did the laundry or looked in the tub, she did not have to know. My grandmother and sister were away at the time. My father swore our maid Lena and I to secrecy. Lena and I then added some more ice, seaweed and salt to the tub, so the that the lobsters would survive for a few more days. Fresh water could not be added, or the lobsters would die. They require salt water.

The lobsters would miraculously appear cooked on our table the next day, with the simple explanation that Lena got them. That was not a lie. The words, "from the laundry tub in the basement," were conveniently left out of the conversation. I think my mother really knew what was going on, but she went along with the charade, because she really loved to eat lobster.

· · · · · · ·

We always took our cat Toots with us when we went to our summer cottage at Amethyst Harbor. The cottage was located about forty-eight km from our home in Fort William. Toots would spend the summer with us at the cottage and she had a great time hunting for birds and mice, bringing them home and then depositing them in my shoes. I always had to check my shoes before I put them on. Toots also liked to wander and explore; sometimes she would disappear for a few days. But she would always return home for a good meal and a bowl of milk. Summer came to an end and it was time to return to our home in Fort William. School began in early September. We were all packed up, ready to go and could not find Toots. My father was waiting in the car and was anxious to get going. We knew that Toots did not like driving in the car, and I thought she was probably hiding. I checked under the beds, inside the woodshed and all of her favorite places. No Toots! After one hour, my father had run out of patience and brought the search to an end by announcing that we were going home and leaving Toots.

I was heartbroken and cried all the way home. By that time my father's blood pressure had returned to normal and he assured me that we would drive back the next weekend and look for Toots. I was not to worry, but I worried all week. We went back to our cottage at Amethyst, not only the next weekend but also the following weekend. There was still no Toots. It was on the second weekend, when we were closing up the cottage for the winter, that my father announced that we were not coming back. Toots was gone, probably run over by a car or killed by a coyote. My dad promised to buy me another cat. I started to cry and pleaded that Toots had probably gone off on one of her trips. Maybe she was visiting another family. But it was no use. My dad would not change his mind. I cried all the way home. If Toots was gone, I did not want another cat. No cat would ever replace Toots. The months passed. Christmas and the New Year followed. Toots had become an all but forgotten memory. It was a Saturday morning in January and as usual it was bitterly cold. The milk bottles on the back steps had popped their caps and the cream had squeezed out of the bottles like toothpaste. Then Toots appeared! She was sitting on our windowsill in her favorite spot, all hunched up with half her ear missing, shivering and mewing to get in from the cold.

Toots had spent the past three months on an incredible forty-eight km journey from our cottage at Amethyst Harbor to our home in Fort William in the middle of winter. We did not know how she did it. The only connecting links were a highway and a railway track. She had to find her way, not only through our city, but also to find her way through the neighboring city of Port Arthur. I thought probably she used the railroad track because it was close to our cottage at Amethyst Harbor, and it also passes close to our home in Fort William. But even that route was difficult, when you consider the many confusing spur lines and railway yards. In addition, there was always the constant freight and passenger traffic travelling both east and west. Marauding coyotes and foxes were also a danger on this miraculous journey home.

When I found toots, I gathered her in my arms and hugged her. She had no strength and had probably lost half of her original body weight.

My grandmother warmed a bowl of milk and some leftover porridge. Even my father had a tear in his eye and announced that Toots was home with us forever. Our friend Sheila Burnford wrote a novel called the Incredible Journey which became a best seller and a popular movie. It is the story about two dogs and a cat that together make an incredible journey across northern Ontario. I think that she was inspired by Toots' incredible journey from Amethyst Harbor to Fort William.

· · · · · · ·

My creative ability emerged early in my life. At the age of eight, I decided that I should build a trailer that I could attach to my bicycle. Bicycle trips and camping overnight in our pup tents was routine. Usually our camping gear, cooking utensils and sleeping bags were carried in backpacks or in bicycle carriers or racks. These were attached to the rear axle and frame of the bike, but we were limited in what they could carry. A trailer was obviously the answer.

My father was very supportive in my endeavors and had a piece of pipe made, which attached to the bike frame and then was curved to fit over the rear wheel and then attached to the trailer. My trailer design was very modernistic with a curved profile cut from nineteen mm thick plywood with a keyhole saw. Weight saving was unfortunately not factored into my design.

Wheel design was another important decision. Bicycle wheels were too big and smaller wagon wheels were not available. I wanted modern looking wheels that looked good with my design. I decided to make my own wheels. I found an abandoned wooden telephone pole and cut four fifty mm thick slices with a swede saw. I then nailed and covered each side with paint-can lids. A hole for the axle was drilled through each wheel. My father provided me with a threaded steel rod axle with nuts on each end. There were no axle casings or bearings. It was wood against steel and that was to be a critical design error. My father could have commented but did not comment. I had to learn the hard way. One summer day my three friends and I decided to camp out and take the trailer. We loaded it up with our gear and attached the trailer to my bike. I got on my bike and tried to move the trailer. It wouldn't move. The trailer was much too heavy, and the load of camping stuff made it worse. We decided to attach two ropes to the trailer and pull together. We were on our way and headed out through Westfort, across the swing bridge on the Kam river and then out Highway 17. Towards Pigeon River and the U S border.

The trailer became increasingly awkward to pull. With no casings, bearings or lubricant, the steel axle was rubbing and wearing down the wood wheel. With no lock nuts on the axles, the nuts would turn and fall off. On one occasion we lost a wheel. It was a disaster. We pulled the trailer for about sixteen km and then camped beside some hills beyond the mental health farm. We spent a terrible night there, A rainstorm dislodged boulders that came thundering down the hill narrowly missing our tents. We could hear wolves howling in the distance. The next day we abandoned the trailer, strapped our gear to our bikes and headed for home. It had been a difficult learning experience- all about axles, casings, bearings and grease.

· · · · · · ·

I said my prayers up until about age eight. My parents would always remind me to say my prayers when I went to bed. I would kneel by the side of my bed, with eyes closed, hands clasped in prayer mode, and then I would recite:

Now I lay me down to sleep,
I pray my Lord my soul to keep.
If I should die before I wake,
I pray my Lord my soul to take.
Please bless my mother, my father and my sister.

This was followed by naming all of my grandparents, aunts and uncles. I always closed with the words:

Please make Grandma's face better.
Amen

None of my friends said their prayers and I had no idea why the Lord would want my soul if I died during the night. In spite of my prayers, Grandma's face did not get better . . .

On Sunday afternoons, I would head back to Isabella School for Sunday School and Bible Study. Mrs. Mills was the teacher who attempted the impossible, in getting us interested in the Bible. I hated it. After receiving my own copy of the Holy Bible at Communion, I never opened it again. I did however, read Hurlbut's Story of the Bible, which my patents had given me as a Christmas present. It was a collection of 168 stories from the Bible with large print and plenty of illustrations. I think it was probably the full-page illustrations that caught my fancy. I read and reread the stories many times without prompting.

I remember the story about the destruction of Sodom and Gomorrah and Lot's wife turning to look back, wishing to return to the sinful city against the angels' instructions and being turned into a pillar of salt. There was a great picture of a female shaped pillar of salt with a flaming city in the distance. Oddly enough, there is a pillar of salt named Lot's wife located near the Dead Sea at Mount Sodom in Israel. My grandmother always had her Bible at her bedside and read it every night before retiring. She never talked or discussed what she had read, and I doubt if she understood what she had read. She did, however, like to boast that she had read the bible three times from cover to cover. For grandma, reading the Bible was a marathon event. Understanding what she had read was not important, bit did ensure her entry to heaven.

· · · · · · ·

We used to build our own go-carts. It was quite easy. All you needed was four wheels, one thick plank, two smaller boards, a soapbox, a nail keg, a piece of rope and a push stick. You fastened the four wheels onto two of the boards and nailed one board to the end of the main plank. Then you drilled matching holes through the front board and the main plank to be connected with a bolt and finished off with the steering rope tied to the ends of the front board. If you wanted to be fancy and were not interested in racing, you could attach the soap box with one side and top removed for use as a seat and the nail keg fastened to the front of the plank for your legs. Tin cans could be added for lights.

The secret to winning was to have a stripped-down cart, a big person pushing and a smaller person steering. I usually chose my friend Mick as my pusher. Go-carts were also built by the next generation. My sons wanted to build a go-cart and I had picked up an empty nail keg in Guelph and stood it in the back seat of our Volkswagen. On the way home to Toronto, I rolled the car over, crushing the roof and it was prevented from becoming completely flattened by the nail keg. I ended up in the Milton hospital with ten stitches in my scalp. I could have been killed in the rollover, but the nail keg saved my life.

· · · · · · ·

Matzo bread is unleavened bread traditionally eaten by Jews during the Passover festival, when bread made with leaven is forbidden according to Jewish religious law. Leaven is yeast or baking powder that makes the bread rise. The Passover officially lasts for one week and usually occurs in April. The eating of unleavened bread is mentioned in Exodus 12.8 and 12.18 of the Bible during the exodus of the Jews from Egypt.

The Petroff family usually had a stock of matzo bread during the entire year. The bread was baked in thin letter-size sheets with rows of perforated holes. It tasted similar to a soda cracker without any salt. I liked matzo bread and would encourage my friend Sol Petroff to sneak into their pantry to get a sheet of matzo. We would sit in the shack, breaking off chunks from the sheet and eating them. It was sacrilegious, but tasty.

· · · · · · ·

The T. Eaton Co. published a very thick mail-order catalogue yearly. Everyone in our family studied it closely. I concentrated on children's toys and sporting goods, particularly at Christmas. I would mark the items that I would like, for reference by my parents, and I was sure to list them in my letter to Santa Claus. Not much has changed. Now I mark up the Lee Valley gardening catalogue and distribute it to my children.

I closely studied the women's brassiere and undergarments section, speculating on what lay hidden. In my study of the human form, I included National Geographic articles on Africa and South America, showing topless women. There were no Playboy magazines or Google search engines in those days. When I was older, I subscribed to Sunbathing, a nudist magazine. It was mailed in a plain brown wrapper and was quite revealing. There were numerous photos of naked men and women of various shapes and sizes playing volleyball, swimming and hiking. I became disenchanted with the shape of the human body and abandoned my studies. I still subscribe to the National Geographic, but I read it for other reasons. The Eaton's catalogue had multiple uses; from providing reading material in the farm outhouse; as a pictorial tool for learning English by early settler; and as goalie pads during hockey games. On occasion, when the toilet paper supply ran out, it was put to other uses.

Eaton's Department store was established by Timothy Eaton in the late1800s and grew into a huge retailing empire, selling everything from clothing to farm implements and employing 70,000 people in stores across Canada. In my lifetime, I would live to see both the peak and the bankruptcy of Eaton's in 1999.

· · · · · · ·

I was very disappointed when my parents gave me a wind-up train for Christmas. All of my friends had Lionel electric trains and I was jealous. The electric trains were powered by small direct current or DC motors. Unlike electric streetcars, the power was transmitted through the rails rather than a trolley wire.

My mother did not fully understand the safety of toys operated with low voltage electric current electricity, but after several years, since none of my friends had been electrocuted, she relented, and I became the owner of my first electric train set. It was great fun. My father provided me with a large sheet of plywood for mounting the track and installing small scale models of landscape including trees and small buildings. With a control switch, I could make the train run backward or forward. There were spur tracks and switches. Freight and passenger cars could be coupled and uncoupled. You could add bridges that raised or lowered and electric lights for the buildings. We stopped playing ping-pong because the train set now sat on the ping-pong table.

Playing with electric trains is addictive and many grown men pursue model train building into their adult life. Both my brother-in-law and a close friend were avid railroaders. I have visited many model train layouts and exhibits in both Canada and the U.S. I have watched grown men, dressed as railroaders having the time of their life, playing in their model train world. Anyone can get hooked up. All aboard!

· · · · · · ·

My sister was named Mugs as a young child and the name stuck with her during her entire life. Her real name was Marguerite. According to my sister, my father came up with the name and the observation that she was just like Maggie Muggins, so he nicknamed her Muggins, which in time became Mugs. Mary Evelyn Grannan was a teacher who taught school in Fredericton, New Brunswick in the 1920. She was a great storyteller and created tales about a young, freckle-faced girl with red hair which she wore in pig tails. She named the girl Maggie Muggins. Her stories then morphed into radio and television shows for the next three decades, after she took a job with CBC. Maggie Muggins was always getting into trouble and I can understand how my father made the connection. Of course, Maggie's appearance bore a sharp resemblance to the Anne of Green Gables character, which Lucy Maud Montgomery had created a decade earlier.

The fact that Mary Evelyn Grannan and my father were about the same age and the fact that she was born and raised in Fredericton, leads me to believe that my father must have known Grannan when she was a young teacher, telling stories to the school children. There had to be some sort of a connection for him to remember Maggie Muggins.

· · · · · · ·

Mr. Hall and his wife lived across the street at 1407. He managed the UK owned Cuthbertson Estate properties in Fort William including the

Cuthbertson Block, a three-story office and commercial building on May Street; Cuthbertson Place, where we lived, plus large tracts of land throughout Fort William. Mr. Hall was a large, stern-faced man with an imposing protruding belly, fastidiously dressed in a suit and vest adorned with a gold chain and watch fob. He was imposing and impressive to his business peers, but we disrespectfully called him "Beer Belly Hall, Beer Belly Hall," when he walked down the street. Then we would giggle and laugh. I'm sure that Mr. Hall did not drink beer, but probably preferred single malt scotch whiskey.

· · · · · · ·

We were always playing board games. The inside board games included Scrabble, Monopoly, Checkers, Chess, Dominoes, Mah Jong, Cribbage and Crokinole. My favorite game was Monopoly.

There were guessing games like I Spy, With My Little Eye and Charades. We had Ouija Boards to communicate with the spiritual world and Tarot cards for foretelling the future. Spelling bees were held both at home and at school.

The only indoor games with any physical activity were ping-pong, arm wrestling and leg wrestling. My father used to practice leg wrestling in the late hours, while partying with his friends. It was embarrassing, seeing my parents behaving like children. Card games were always popular and included: Go Fish, Hearts, Spades, Solitaire, Spider, Poker, Whist, Euchre, Cribbage and Bridge. Spelling bees were usually reserved for the classroom, but occasionally we would have them at home.

Outdoors we played marbles, can-the-can, hide and seek, tag, hopscotch and skipping. We all learned to bowl using both five and ten pins, and in the winter we curled. Croquet was also popular. We played soft ball, hard ball, badminton and tennis in the summer. I preferred badminton.

Game playing is not only essential for kids, but it is also important for adults. In our modern lives, many of us focus so heavily on work and family commitments, that we never have time for pure fun. I would urge my readers to play. Play bridge with some friends, throw a frisbee or make a snowman with your kids. Play does not have to be competitive like golf or bowling. Calm yourself, turn on the music and dance with your wife, ski down a snow slope, play fetch with your dog. Enjoy!

• • • • • • •

From age six to ten, I was involved making model airplanes out of balsa wood and tissue paper. The planes came in kits, complete with glue, colored tissue and sheets of thin balsa wood imprinted with the various aircraft components. I would carefully cut the balsa wood using one of my father's razor blades and then glue the components onto a skeleton frame of the aircraft. The colored tissue was used to provide a skin over the skeleton frame. After coating the frame with a thin layer of glue, I would spray and dampen the tissue paper and spread it over the frame. After the tissue had dried, it would shrink and tighten up, creating a nice smooth surface. Power for flight was provided by means of a rubber band attached to the propeller and to the end of the frame. By rotating the propeller, the elastic would twist and tighten, storing up energy.

Flight tests were conducted in Vickers Park with mixed results. In some cases, the rubber band broke. For those models, making it into the air, many crashed by losing poweand then nosediving into the ground, or getting caught by a gust of wind and ending up in the trees. With the persistence of the Wright Brothers, who preceded us by thirty years, we rebuilt our aircraft and tried again. The experience did teach us that failure followed by persistence brings success.

"If you don't succeed, try, try again."

• • • • • • •

In addition to receiving a generous salary as chief engineer of the Great Lakes Paper Company, my father and the mill manager enjoyed many company perks. GLP employees would regularly appear at Cuthbertson Place to cut the lawn, shovel snow, spade the garden and trim the hedge. My dad added a two-story addition to our house in the late 1930s. The GLP chief carpenter worked for weeks finishing the house. The new second floor bedroom was for my parents, providing extra sleeping space for my grandmother, now a permanent resident. The first floor of the addition was a den finished in Philippine mahogany with a complete wall of shelves, full of books my father never read. The basement of the addition was my room, first used for play and later as my study. I just took my father's perks for granted and was envied by my peers for escaping the home maintenance jobs.

· · · · · · ·

In Grade Six, I can remember having a crush on a girl who attended another school. Shirley Perry lived nearby on Harkness Street and we never met or exchanged a word I would ride by her house on my bicycle, hoping for an encounter. It never happened.

Helen Olsen was another matter. Her father made the name famous with the creation of Olsen's Fly Dope which he cooked up on their kitchen stove. The recipe was never disclosed, but it did work. Helen and I were in the same class and exchanged Valentine cards and passed secret notes about class activities. Our opinions about teachers were shared. We both disliked Mr. McCoy, who taught geography and smelled of nicotine and we both liked Miss Brent, who taught art. Helen flamed out for me in later years with the addition of braces, eyeglasses and twenty pounds of excess weight.

· · · · · · ·

The arrival of my grandmother to live with us on a permanent basis ended the necessity of having the Galliant sisters as maids. Grandma ran the house, including the preparation of all the meals, washing the clothes, pressing and ironing. Heavy work including cleaning, waxing and polishing was done by a cleaning lady, once a week.

Grandma was constantly baking bread, biscuits, pies, cakes and tarts. She pickled and preserved all manner of fruit, vegetables, jams and jellies. She did it all without a cookbook. A pot of soup with the latest leftovers usually simmered on the stove. There was always a constant supply of fudge, toffee and peanut brittle carefully squirreled away.

She was always shooshing me out of the kitchen for snitching her daily offerings. My practice of drinking milk from the bottle and making brown sugar or ketchup sandwiches did not impress her. With the advantage of better eyesight, I also tormented her by finding worms in the raspberries, after she had carefully picked through them.

There was a ritual in our meals, with oatmeal porridge and brown sugar for breakfast, stew on Wednesday, fish with French fries on Friday, baking on Saturday, bacon and eggs for Sunday breakfast and roast beef and potatoes for Sunday supper. A different custard or pudding would appear at every lunch. We were spoiled rotten by my grandma.

· · · · · · ·

My parents regularly took my sister and I with them on trips to various parts of Canada and the U.S. Their goal was to educate and introduce us to the amazing world around us. Our goal was to escape from school, for a couple of weeks, while our peer group stayed at home. We travelled to Florida in the winter to tan on the beach and swim in the ocean, to Wyoming and Montana to observe the geothermal wonders of Yellowstone National Park and to our roots in Lorneville and Saint John, N.B., to visit our relatives and sample the treats from the Bay of Fundy.

In the summer of 1939, they took us to the New York World's Fair. The NYWF was the first exposition to be based on the future, with an opening slogan of "Dawn of a New Day" and we were introduced to the "World of Tomorrow."

There were a host of new products including fluorescent lights, automatic dishwashers, electronic voice machines and rotary milk parlors for milking, bathing, and drying cows. There were automatic baking machines, electric typewriters and calculators. Nylon fabric, the View-Master and Scentovision were introduced. I fell in love with the variety of rides that where available, including the Flyer Train and Aquacades.

The most memorable event of the New York trip for me was the Automat Restaurant. It had been around for a long time and there were hundreds of restaurants all around the city. It consisted of banks of compartments with glass doors containing sandwiches, pies, cakes, hot dishes and coffee. You simply dropped a nickel in a slot. Opened the door and took out your meal.

The educational value of the trip was not lost, however. I did come away with some knowledge of the creativity of my fellow man and the thought that I could become part of it.

· · · · · · ·

After my cat Toots died, my parents purchased an Irish terrier as a pet. I called him Rory, but his official pedigree name was Ballycliffe Blimp. Rory was colored golden red and had no other markings. He had a bushy beard with eyebrows to match and two reddish ears both lopped forward and a docked tail. I don't know whether it was Rory's Irish heritage or his status as a pedigree dog, but Rory was oversexed and humped everything in sight. Human legs were his specialty. Small children could be knocked over and frightened. I had to restrain him on a leash when a local female dog was in heat. To my knowledge Rory's sexual enthusiasm never resulted in any local puppies with Irish ancestry.

My mother made rules for both child and pet behavior. Rory was confined to the kitchen, because she did not want dog hair in other parts of the house. Rory would test the rule and lie on the kitchen floor with one paw across the hall door threshold. I would give one command "Rory", and he would withdraw the paw. He really gave himself away one morning when my father found the door to the dining room swinging back and forth.

Rory was definitely my dog and would be my companion all during my high school years. My sister, being older, was more interested in two-legged male humans, rather than four-legged animals. Rory passed on when I was at University and it would be a dozen years before another pet arrived in my life . . .

When you grow up in Fort William, you learn how to ski at an early age. I started out with snowshoes and then graduated to skis. The skis were made from wood rather than the composition plastics used today and were fastened to your feet with a steel toe cleat and a buckle at the heel. The poles were made of bamboo, with metal hoops attached to the bottom of the pole and leather straps attached to the handles at the top.

We skied at the Fort William Ski Club on Mount McKay. On Saturday morning we would begin early and catch a streetcar ride out to Highway 69, followed by a one km cross-country trek to the ski hill. If no one had preceded us, we would have to break the trail through the freshly fallen snow. After arriving at the clubhouse and fortified by hot chocolate, we would spend the rest of the morning compacting the snow on the nursery slopes by tamping it with our skis. By noon we were ready to ski.

In the early days there were no tows to take us up the hill to the higher slopes. This predicament was solved by the installation of the first rope tows powered by electricity. A family friend and electrical engineer from the Great Lakes Paper Company designed the tow. His sons took turns punching our tow cards, allowing us to be pulled 100 m up the hill.

The rope tow was eventually succeeded by steel cables with hanging rods and circular plates attached. You straddled the plate with your crotch and hung on to the hanger rod. The device was called the Poma-Lift and was eventually replaced by T-bars and chair lifts. Little do the children of today, who are driven to a hill covered with manufactured snow and groomed by machine, and then put on their special boots and composition skis know about the early days of skiing.

More slopes were cleared and groomed as the ski club grew and a ski jump was added. A new downhill run was cut from the peak of the mountain providing a descent of 250 m in a length of 1400 m. The prime factor for good skiing is snow, and Fort William had an abundance of the white stuff. The fact that it did not melt, and the absence of icy slopes and piercing winds made conditions perfect. These were the reasons why the Fort William Ski Club was chosen for the Dominion Ski Meet of 1939.

Mount McKay is located south of Fort William, rising 271 m above Lake Superior. The Ojibwa Indians called it Thunder Mountain and used it for sacred ceremonies. The mountain is part of the local reservation and access is allowed on a toll-road up to the first ledge, built by and controlled by the Indians. Mount McKay is composed of a soft shale base, capped by a protective hard igneous rock. Unknown to our parents we would climb up the shale slopes to the first ledge. As we climbed, large stones were dislodged, narrowly missing the climbers below. Our parents were not aware of these ascents until later in life. Once we arrived at the first ledge, there was a panoramic view of Fort William, the Kaministiquia River and the city harbor. In the distance you could see the city of Port Arthur backed by the smoky hills; out on Lake Superior, the Sleeping Giant of Thunder Cape lay on his back where he had been for thousands of years, waiting patiently for his wife Nanna Bijou, whom he had angered, to return. The Welcome Islands, Pie Island and in the distance Isle Royale and the United States territory can be seen.

· · · · · · ·

The Sleeping Giant is a rock formation on Sibley Peninsula which resembles a giant lying on his back when viewed from Fort William and Port Arthur from the west. Its remarkable steep cliffs are among the highest in Ontario. One Ojibwa legend identifies the giant as Nanna Bijou, who was turned into stone, when the secret of a rich silver mine, now known as Silver Islet, was disclosed to white men. I prefer another more romantic legend that the giant is lying on his back waiting patiently for his estranged wife to return. The sleeping giant has become a symbol of Fort William and Port Arthur, now renamed as Thunder Bay. My eldest son used the profile, when he created a design for my wife's family reunion in 1996. During a popular vote for naming the Seven Wonders of Canada, the Sleeping Giant came first, followed by Niagara Falls, The Bay of Funday, Nahanni National Park Reserve, The Northern Lights, The Canadian Rockies and the Cabo Trail. Ultimately the Sleeping Giant was not selected by a panel of judges, who decided their vote by geographic and poetic criteria. The six judges chose The Canoe, Niagara Falls, Pier Twenty-One in Halifax, The Rockies, Old Quebec City and Prairie Skies. Over one million Canadians, including me, who had voted for The Sleeping Giant, felt slighted.

· · · · · · ·

Silver Islet is a small rock island and community located at the tip of the Sibley Peninsula. The peninsula stretches out from the mainland for fifty-one km into Lake Superior, creating a body of water called Thunder Bay. The Sleeping Giant rock formation forms the southern-most extension of the peninsula. My friend Mick's family rented a cottage in the Silver Islet community and I was a frequent visitor. I was always fascinated by the story of the silver mine. A rich vein of pure silver was discovered on the small islet at the end of the peninsula in the late 1800s. The islet was quite small and only two decimal four metres above the waters of Lake Superior. Wooden breakwaters were constructed to expand the island and to protect the mineshaft, increasing the size of the islet by ten times. The mine produced millions of dollars of silver as the shaft was sunk deeper and deeper, reaching a depth of 384 m. Surrounded by water, the mine had to be continuously pumped out by coal-fired engines. The mineshaft eventually flooded when a shipment of coal did not arrive at the end of the shipping season and the mine was never reopened.

· · · · · · ·

When I visited my grandmother at her Keewatin home in the summer, the only person to play with was Jimmy Craig. Jimmy lived in a house down the hill and was three years younger. Our families made a great effort to promote the friendship. Jimmy and I were completely incompatible. In addition to the age difference, Jimmy was interested in music and dressing up in girl's clothes. I was interested in crushing rocks up on the hill and using the material to build roads for my trucks. Quite frankly, we disliked each other, and the relationship continued in adult life. Jimmy went on to become an accomplished musician, coach and conductor, having trained in Winnipeg, London, England and Rome. He became the musical director of the University of Toronto Opera Department, with a large repertoire of operas under his direction. I pursued my engineering career and although we both lived in the same city, we never talked or socialized.

· · · · · · ·

I was always pleased when my father brought home bags of raw pulp used in the production of newsprint. I would wet it down and use it to create roads and landscapes for my toy cars and trucks. I used the new basement addition of the house, which had a concrete floor, to create my play world.

Entry to the room was through the furnace room. The trouble was that pulp is vegetable matter, which grows moldy with time, turns a purplish green color and starts to smell. Since the basement was rarely visited by my parents and since I looked after the furnace, my parents were not aware of the mold or the smell. It was our maid Lena that blew the whistle and I had to shovel the mess out.

· · · · · · ·

There was an abundance of cordwood in Northern Ontario, and it was used for building everything from stacked housing and roads to bridge decks and sidewalks. The sidewalk on Cuthbertson Place ran along the north side of the road and was constructed using a wood deck supported by concrete walls. The neat thing about the sidewalk was that you could crawl underneath. I am not sure how we gained entry to the space, but it was a great place for hiding and then scaring the daylights out of someone, preferably a girl walking above, and yelling. "Beware, beware, I can see your underwear."

· · · · · · ·

Caribou Island was located about one and a half miles southeast of our cottage on the North Bay of Amethyst Harbor. It is a remarkable island, home to white-tail deer, peregrine falcons and bald eagles. Oddly enough, there are no caribou. High rocky bluffs face the mainland shore, and we could canoe from our cottage to the face of the sheer bluffs. There were gorges cut through the rock by streams, allowing us to climb to the top. There was always the danger of loose rock being dislodged and hitting a climber. It was dangerous and my parents had no idea of what was going on. Once we had climbed to the top of the bluffs, we would head to a small lake for lunch and a swim. In later years, Pat and I and some friends made the same trip and we all skinny dipped in the cool water. It was my first introduction and pleasure of swimming with naked women.

I was happy to read some sixty years later that sixty-four hectares of the south shore had been purchased by the Nature Conservancy of Ontario, preventing the island from being taken over by cottagers.

· · · · · · ·

I think that every young child likes candy and has a favourite candy store. My source of supply was located on nearby Franklin Street. I would save up my pennies and head off to buy jawbreakers, suckers and jellybeans. When Pat and I had the condo at Cranberry Village in Collingwood, our grandchildren would visit, and we would give them each a dollar to spend at the local Candy Factory. They would walk to the store and take forever to study the various varieties of candy available to fill up their bag. It was always a highlight of their visit and one that they will still remember. Twenty years later, the Collinwood Candy Factory is still in operation and is now conveniently located across from the local high school.

· · · · · · ·

The Argyle II was Kenora's water bus for almost fifty years. It was one of the last coal-fired steamships on the Lake of the Woods. For decades, prior to the completion of the Norman and Keewatin bridges, it was the only way for goods and people to travel between the three communities of Kenora, Norman and Keewatin. It was also used for daily two-hour tours of the Lake of the Woods and for bringing people to the local playground at Coney Island Beach.

The Argyle II was docked in the harbor close to my grandmother's house. When we visited each summer, I took frequent trips. Captain Fraser was a cousin, and the fare was reasonable. I particularly liked the Kenora trip and passing through Devil's Gap. Sometime in the past, a giant spirit rock was painted with a large face that looked like the devil. The Argyle II was taken out of service in 1985 and was used as a summer home by the McLaughlin family. The boat had deteriorated badly, so that only the hull remained.

In recent years, a local effort to salvage the hull and tow it back to Kenora was successful. The Argyle II Historic Trust was incorporated under the direction of a group pf volunteers with the aim of restoring the ship and using it as an attraction to raise money for charity.

· · · · · · · ·

The St. Joseph's Residential School in Fort William was affiliated with the Roman Catholic Church and was operated by the Sisters of St. Joseph of Sault Ste. Marie. The school was originally established as an orphan asylum at the nearby Fort William Indian Reserve, and was moved to Franklin Street, a short distance from our home on Cuthbertson Place, to operate as a residential school.

This was a black period in Canadian history, when Indian children were forced to leave their parental homes to reside in residential schools. Ostensibly this was to Canadianize and educate the children, but it alienated both the children and their parents. The children were brainwashed in Catholic dogma, and in many cases were abused by priests and nuns alike.

They lived in the school for ten months of the year and were only allowed home for two months in the summer.

Over 300 children lived in the huge four-story residential school on Franklin Street, with the church and high school conveniently located next door. The Indian children played in a high fenced area at the rear of the church. Barbed wire at the top of the fence, discouraged them from leaving. As a youngster, I had no understanding of why the Indian children were in the residential school. Only recently, with the creation of the Canadian Truth and Reconciliation Commission in 2008, and my studies of the Inuit culture in Northern Canada, did I become aware of the residential school problems.

It is interesting to note, that by 2015, many of the Anglican and Catholic bishops have apologized for the residential school fiasco, but Pope Francis has remained silent.

· · · · · · ·

When you grow up and go to the movies with matinee idols such as Gene Autrey, Roy Rogers and the Lone Ranger, you had to have a toy gun, preferably a cap gun. There were many kinds of guns from small pistols to rifles. The pistols were generally in three styles, the semi-automatic revolver with a rotating cylinder carrying a disc of percussion caps; a mock revolver that looked like a regular revolver but opened to load a roll of caps; and later on, toy guns that shott plastic bullets using a spring. It was great playing cowboys and Indians and having shootouts at the Lone Star Saloon.

. . . .

My father and I never made it in the male bonding department. I'm not talking about family picnics or vacations together, I'm talking about spending quality time together, teaching, learning and communicating. My father was a very busy man when I was growing up in the thirties and forties. By the time I was a young man, I lost all contact due to his debilitating stroke in 1951.

Mick's father on the other hand, took time to bond. He took us fishing for brook trout. He knew and had access to the properties of many farmer, who had secured a loan from his bank. He knew every local stream on the farms which contained brook trout. He taught me how to bait a hook and how to launch flies. He taught me to be patient and wait for the fish to take the bait. When I visited my grandmother in Keewatin, my uncles would take me fishing for pickerel in the Lake of the Woods. They taught me how to gut and fillet a fish. I never went fishing with my father. His fishing trips were with other businessmen in a motorized launch, trolling for lake trout with a rod in one and a glass of scotch in the other.

Mick 's father taught me how to golf and how to hold a club and swing. He was a member of the Fort William Golf and Country Club and regularly took Mick and I with him. My father, on the other hand would go golfing and lose his temper when he hooked or sliced the ball. Golfing was a competition for him He played to win. I would play golf with pleasure during my teens and early twenties, ultimately putting my clubs away in later years, feeling that it was a waste of time. My friend Mick continued to golf, with pleasure into his eighties.

JUST ME

My father taught me how to play bridge, how to arm wrestle, and leg wrestle. We played Ping-Pong together in the basement and went bowling. But it was always about winning. We attended baseball games and hockey games together. My father liked spectator sports and I preferred to participate. Mick's father taught me how to garden and sowed the seeds for a lifetime of personal gardening. In retirement, I became a Master Gardener and Floral Judge. I regret that my father and I had not been closer. We just failed to bond.

. . . .

I spent seven years in Isabella Public School and skipped Grade Four. The old red masonry school was located on the corner of Isabella and Franklin Streets, a short distance from my home. It was close enough that I walked home for lunch during a one and a half-hour lunch break. There were three entrances to the school, a girl's entrance, a boy's entrance and a front entrance that was rarely used. The school yard was divided, and the boys and girls did not play together at recess.

The classrooms were well lit with blackboards along two walls and a cloakroom at the front of the classroom. We all sat at wooden desks mounted on cast iron frames bolted to the floor. There was a seat attached to the front of the desk for the student in front of you. There was a circular inkwell on each desk and a groove for holding your pencils. If there was a girl sitting at the desk n front, you could dip the end of her pigtail in the inkwell. Books were stored on a shelf below. Pencils and ink pens with nibs were used for printing and writing.

We spent our early years learning how to print, and later we practiced penmanship by following the instructions of the teacher, who used chalk on the blackboard. Classes regularly began with a Christian prayer, a practice not followed today, because of our multi-racial population. Misdemeanors such as laughing, passing notes or causing a disturbance were rewarded with banishment to the cloakroom or standing in a corner. The ultimate punishment was an after four detention and a half hour, repetitively writing a mea culpa on the blackboard, followed by cleaning chalk from the dirty brushes. Despite my frequent absence from school due to sickness, I always had good grades and was quite surprised to see my grades drop after starting high school with larger classes and much greater competition. In looking through The Memory Box, I found my report card for 1941 to 1942 Grade VII with twenty-two A, twenty-seven B and three C grades. The teacher remarks ranged from good to exceptional. .

・・・・・・・

With my civil engineering roots, I have always been interested in bridges and ended up designing a few. Fort William was an ideal location for a bridge lesson. There were two bridges that crossed he Kaministiquia River. One was a bascule or jackknife bridge and the other was a swing bridge. The jackknife bridge linked Mission Island with the city and was constructed by the Canadian Pacific Railway. The bridge had a lower deck for trains and an upper deck for personal, and commercial vehicles. The bridge required very little power to operate. It was like a giant teeter-totter with a huge counterweight on one end and the extended deck on the other end. The disadvantage was that the vehicular approaches had to be elevated, making it unsuitable for many locations. The bridge was eventually closed to vehicular traffic but is still used for rail traffic.

The swing bridge connecting the Mount McKay area and west Fort William accommodated railway, streetcar and vehicular traffic. It was a two-span structure powered by a rotating hub. Although more costly to operate, it did allow for grade-level construction and the passage of ships on both sides of the hub.

・・・・・・・

Malcolm Gladwell, in his novel titled David and Goliath, wrote that innovators shared three traits of openness, conscientiousness and agreeableness. Innovators have to be open. They have to be able to imagine things that others cannot and to challenge their own preconceptions. An innovator, who has a brilliant idea, but lacks the discipline and persistence to carry it out, is merely a dreamer. Innovators also disagree and take social risks that others do not approve of. They don't agree with the usual practice of conforming and seeking the approval of others.

Traditionally a fireplace screen is made out of coarse woven wire, mounted in a metal frame that is painted black. My father made a screen out of thick, heat resisting glass, mounted on two supports made of stainless steel. I inherited the screen and used it for our living room fireplace. The screen was innovative. Imitation wood fireplaces contained cast iron logs illuminated with a conventional white light bulb. My father created a copper lined fireplace for the den with artificial cast-iron logs and a red-light source. He devised a lightweight metal propeller, which was attached to the light bulb. Heat from the bulb created warm convection currents, which made the propeller to rotate, casting flickering shadows on the reflective copper lining. The fire was realistic enough that guests would flick their cigar and cigarette ash into the fireplace.

I think that I must have inherited some of my father's innovative DNA, which in later life led to my interest in product development and a string of patents.

. . . .

Every young boy and even older men love fireworks. I was no exception. As a youngster, the cheapest firework that we could buy was a string of thin twelve mm long Chinese firecrackers, which we called "Chinks." We would have to wait for an event like Dominion Day, later changed to Canada Day, on the first of July, for our parents to buy a more expensive assortment of Roman candles, cones, rockets, pin wheels, and sparklers. There was an assortment of cakes, barrages, and bombshells. The highlight of the evening was always the burning schoolhouse.

Fireworks also led me to explore the creation of smoke bombs, and pipe bombs. I had a toy chemistry set at the time, which provided me with a source pf ammonium nitrate. When I mixed it with sugar in a stove pot at low heat, the sugar would caramelize and turn into a mixture with the consistency of peanut butter. I would then pour it into a discarded toilet paper tube with one end capped with Scotch tape or electrical tape. When the tube was full, I inserted a fuse made from string and then capped the open end with tape.

Since smoke bombs were a little tame, I graduated into making pipe bombs. These were much more dangerous. Real pipe bombs are made with short lengths of steel pipe, threaded and capped at both ends, and filled with a sealed glass vial of vinegar and small rocks or nails to break the vial, topped off with baking soda, when thrown, on impact the vial is broken by the rocks or nails and the liquid vinegar mixes, reacts and expands with great explosive force, blowing the pipe and contents into tiny fragments. My pipe bombs were not as lethal. I merely used an empty baby food can, added some baking soda, poured some vinegar into the open end and then ran. It created a great explosion and the can sailed over the house. Years later my neighbor and I recreated this experiment using a short piece of steel pipe capped on one end, but open on the other end. We set up the bomb in the middle of the street. Much to the joy of my sons and neighborhood children, the pipe sailed over the hydro wires strung across the street. Our wives quickly intervened. We were setting a bad example. The demonstration was never repeated.

· · · · · · · ·

From early childhood, I always slept with the door cracked open and the hall light left on. I was afraid of the dark. I still sleep with a nightlight on in the bedroom, because it allows me to see when I get up in the middle of the night when I go to the bathroom, or am I still afraid of the dark?

Between the ages of five and ten, I suffered from night terrors. These were not nightmares. My night terrors were animated. I would sit bolt upright in bed, thrashing about and screaming. My eyes would be wide open with a look of fear or panic on my face. I would sweat and my pajamas would be soaked. My parents or the maid would quiet me down and dry me off. I would wake in the morning with no memory of the event.

Sleepwalking also occurred during these events and I would be found walking through the house and even going outside. It was very unpredictable Again there would be no memories.

My friend Jim Burrow suffered from a similar sleep walking disorder. On one occasion he was visiting our summer cottage at Amethyst Harbor. The cottage was located on a high cliff overlooking South Bay. We decided to camp out overnight in a tent, In the middle of the night, Jim appeared at the entrance to the tent soaking wet, bruised and bleeding. He said that he had woken up in the waters of South Bay harbor. Apparently, he had walked in his sleep and fallen from the high cliff at the cottage into the water. There is only one way to get out of the water and that is by way of a concrete dock built at the base of the cliff with a wood stair leading up to our cottage. We checked the dock and sure enough, Jim had left a trail of wet footprints and blood. If Jim had swum any other way, he would have drowned.

There are many psychiatric theories about sleep walking, dreams, night terrors and nightmares, which are based on stress, a traumatic event, sleep apnea or sickness. I had none of these disorders. I was, however, a voracious reader of adventure books including The Hardy Boys by Franklin W. Dixon, science fiction novels by Jules Verne and outer space stories by Philip Knowlan. I think that my night terrors were probably caused by my reading and my imagination, and not by any anxiety or stress in my life.

· · · · · · ·

It is strange what you remember, but I can remember my parents sitting in the den, holding hands, listening to Jeanette McDonald and Nelson Eddy on the radio singing Indian Love Call.

When I'm calling you

Oo-Oo-Oo-Oo
Will you answer too Oo-Oo- Oo- Oo

They also liked:
Ah sweet mysteries of life,
At last I've found you

THOMAS MCCAVOUR

·······

It was Sunday, September 1, 1939, and I was awakened by the cries of a newsboy shouting, "We are at war." My father rushed to the front door and grabbed the paper in one hand and tipped the boy with a quarter. The front page of the Times-Journal had only four words, WE ARE AT WAR.

World War II was a global war that lasted from 1939 to 1945, though related conflicts started earlier. It involved the vast majority of the world nations, including all of the great powers, eventually forming two opposing alliances, the Allies and the Axis. It was the most widespread war in history, and directly involved more than 100 million people from over thirty different countries.

In a state of "total war," the major participants threw their entire, economic, industrial and scientific capabilities behind the war effort. Marked by the mass death of civilians, including the holocaust in which approximately six million people were killed, and the strategic bombing of large industrial and population centers, including the atomic bombings of Hiroshima and Nagasaki, killing over 100,000 people. These events made World War II the deadliest conflict in human history.

As a teenager, I did not appreciate either the scope or the true meaning of war. I joined Army Cadets while in high school, my father was chairman of nine Victory Loan drives, my cousin Buzz Lamb was shot down over Hamburg, my friend Jack Nugent joined the air force, Micks' brother Steve joined he army, we had regular Sunday dinners with men from the local Air Training School, there was always war bond staff at our house, my father plotted the progress of the war using huge war maps with stick pins and we sang war songs around the piano, including *The Maple Leaf Forever, There'll Always The Be An England, Over There and Ma! I Miss Your Apple Pie*. During the five years of the war, I was too absorbed in my own high school life. I just did not appreciate the scope of mass killing or the devastation of entire cities that was occurring outside of Canada. . .. . .

Within two months of the outbreak of war, Canadian troops were in the United Kingdom and witnessed the evacuation of Dunkirk and the English Channel ports. Canadians were dispatched to Hong Kong in time to meet the Japanese invasion, only to surrender two years later. We were losing the war on both fronts. There were major battles to be fought.

The Dieppe raid on the northwestern shore of France was a complete disaster with 1000 Canadian men killed and 2000 taken prisoner. Allied forces landed in Sicily and battled their way northward in Italy, ultimately costing the lives of nearly 6000 Canadians. In the air, Canadians flew bombers over Germany and fought air battles with German Messerschmitt fighter aircraft.

Back home, Pat's family had moved from Saskatchewan to Fort William early in the war. Her father and her older sister were both involved with the war effort, working at the Canadian Car Company, making Hawker Hurricane aircraft. In the summer my friend Mick worked on an old belt-driven lathe at Northern Engineering, making shell casings for bombs. There were jobs for everyone. The young men were all at war.

· · · · · · ·

The British Commonwealth Air Training Plan was a major program for training Allied air crews from the United Kingdom, New Zealand, Australia and Canada during World War II and was administered by the Canadian Government. Schools and facilities were set up in 231 locations across Canada. Fort William was selected because it had an existing airport that could be used.

An Elementary Flying Training School was established in Fort William. Two-wing Tiger Moths were used for training. After practicing in a mechanical training machine, this was the airmen's first experience of actually taking off, flying and landing an aircraft. During the war, there were always planes in the air and the occasional forced landing or crash.

Every Sunday night my parents would invite a group of airmen to our home for a few drinks, followed by a roast beef and apple pie dinner. After dinner we all headed for the living room and gathered around the piano to sing songs from the latest sheet music. I don't know if it was the dinner, the music or my good-looking sister that attracted the airmen, but the dinner parties were a great success.

My cousin Buzz Lamb was one of the airmen who spent time with us. Buzz's plane was shot down over Hamburg, Germany. My brother-in-law Owen Roberts flew a Lancaster bomber during the war, Mick's brother Steve served with the Canadian army in Italy and my friend Jack Nugent joined the air-force, but never saw action.

· · · · · · ·

After the start of the war with Japan in 1941, the Canadian Government sent 22,000 British Columbia residents of Japanese descent to relocation camps far from the coast. The reason given was intense public demand for removal, and fear of espionage or sabotage. In reflection, it was a knee-jerk reaction. It was completely unjust and undemocratic, to tear people away from homes and businesses that had taken a lifetime to build. The government ignored reports from the RCMP and Canadian Military, that said most of the Japanese were law-abiding citizens and not a threat. As a Canadian, I am embarrassed about our role in this wartime event. It has taken a long time for reconciliation to take place. In 1988 Prime Minister Brian Mulroney apologized on behalf of the Canadian Government. In 2013, during the designated Year of Reconciliation and seventy-one years after the event, the City of Vancouver and the Anglican Church of Canada both apologized for their role in the affair.

· · · · · · ·

Canada used War Saving Certificates and Victory Bonds to fund the expenses of war. War Savings Certificates were first sold in the 1940's by banks, authorized dealers and even by volunteers through door-to-door campaigns. The maturity period was seven years, and the return was five dollars for every four dollars, with a maximum investment of six hundred dollars. The government quickly realized that the maturity time was too short and the spending limit too low. They introduced Victory Bonds maturing in six to fourteen years at yields of one and a half percent for short term and three percent for long term and no limit for purchasing.

Wars are expensive and Victory Bonds enabled the government to finance the war.

During the war my father was the chairman of nine of the eleven Victory Bond drives. The Great Lakes Paper Company volunteered his services at no charge, but he was still expected to function as chief engineer of the company. I had a similar role when I headed up the 1957 United Appeal in Guelph, Ontario.

The Great Lakes Paper Company donated my father's time and he delegated some of his work to others or merely postponed it for the duration of the drive. He was constantly motivating people to sell the war bonds. He was always on the go and our house was populated with organizers who were sent from Toronto, and members of the community who planned and implemented each campaign. In reflection the Victory Bond drives took a terrible toll on family relationships and my father's health. My father chaired eight loan drives during the war and one after the war. His only reward were fond memories and nine commemorative plaques, which eventually ended up forgotten and gathering dust in the loft of our garage. I think that the stress of running the campaigns and handling his regular job at GLPC took its toll on my father's health. A perforated abdomen in 1948 was followed by a stroke in 1951, permanently ended his engineering career and his ability to communicate.

· · · · · · ·

Mathew Halton was Canada's voice at war, He was a war correspondent, working for the Canadian Broadcasting Corporation and became famous for his accounts of battles during World War II. His voice brought the war into the living rooms of Canadians. My father was a great fan and was absolutely thrilled when he met Halton during the Seventh Victory Loan Campaign. It was 1944, the Allies had landed in Normandy and battles with the Germans were being fought in Belgium and France. Halton had reluctantly left the battlefield to spearhead the Seventh Victory Loan Campaign back in Canada. He travelled across Canada for fund raising events in theatres, civic auditoriums, hotels and arenas My father introduced him during a Fort William rally at the Orpheum Theatre. I write these memoirs having recently read *Dispatches from the Front – The Life of Mathew Halton* written by his son David Halton.

· · · · · · ·

Radio was becoming quite popular, and it was filled with news from the battlefront and popular war songs of the time. We would sing them with great enthusiasm at home, school, or church. I still remember some of the lyrics.

We'll meet again
Don't know where
Don't know when
But I know we'll meet again some sunny day

When the lights go on again, all over the world
And the boys come home again, all over the world
And rain and snow is all that will fall from the skies above
A kiss won't mean "goodbye" but hello to love
When the lights go on again.

Other songs included:

There'll Be Bluebirds Over, The White Cliffs of Dover, I'll Be Seeing You, and *There'll Always Be An England.*

One of the most popular songs was a German love song titled *Lily Marlene*. It became popular with soldiers of both sides and was sung in both German and English by Marlene Dietrich a German-born singer and movie actress.

Underneath the lantern by the barrack gate
Darling I remember, the way you used to wait
'Twas there that you whispered tenderly
That you loved me
You'd always be

JUST ME

*My Lili of the lamplight My
own Lili Marlene*

. . . .

The Canadian Army Cadet Program has a history dating back to 1879. Their motto, Acer Pori means As the Maple, so the Sapling. The aim of the cadet program was to develop in youth the attributes of good citizenship and leadership; promote physical fitness; and stimulate the interest of youth in the sea, land and air activities of the Canadian Forces. These were all very noble aims, but I think that the real aim was to brainwash youth into volunteering for the Canadian armed forces. There were Army, Air and Nav Cadet programs in existence when I attended high school. They were not mandatory, but I can think of no one in our school who was not a member of a cadet program. I joined the Army Cadets during my first year in high school in the fall of 1943. In recognition of the role of former cadets to the ongoing war effort, His Majesty King George VI granted the "Royal" prefix to the Canadian Army, Air and Sea Cadets. It is estimated that nearly 230,000 former cadets served in His Majesty's forces during the Second World War.

In spring, summer, and fall, we trained at the local high school grounds. In the winter, we trained at the local armory. We learned all of the elements of drilling and practicing marksmanship at the rifle range. Army Cadet training also triggered he end to my Boy Scout career. The two were incompatible. We had to line up for inspection. Our shoes had to be polished, uniforms spotless and pressed with every button gleaming. We also had to stand at attention, waiting for the inspection to end. I can remember one of our innovative members was caught during inspection, with a bottle of pop hidden in his uniform and connected to his mouth by a long plastic tube. He was immediately expelled.

Years later, I can remember visiting my son at his Duncan home. His son Bryan had just joined Air Cadets and I was with him for his first night of training. When I questioned his wisdom in joining Air Cadets rather than Sea Cadets, since he lived on an island surrounded by water, he advised me that he chose Air Cadets, because they had the smartest uniforms. In the summer he attended Army Cadet programs. I suppose that was just part of the evolutionary process. Eventually he completed his tri-service experience and joined the British Royal Navy, where he became a Commander.

· · · · · · ·

Movies during WW II were thinly disguised propaganda stories meant to stimulate your patriotism and support for the war effort. They were usually about battles involving our armed forces and after heroic efforts, we always won. There were spy dramas and plots by our secret agents to bomb, assassinate or poison the bad guys, who were always German, Japanese or Italian.

There were a few movies that were comedies. Bob Hope starred in a series of "Road" movies with Bing Crosby and Dorothy Lamour including, Road to Singapore, Road to Zanzibar and Road to Morocco. Comedians Abbott and Costello and Laurel and Hardy also made war movies. The only movie I actually remember was Mrs. Miniver, starring Oscar winning Greer Garson and Gregory Peck.

· · · · · · ·

Alf and Jessie Hanigan were our next-door neighbors Their home at 1414 Cuthbertson Place was a detached bungalow. Our house and their house were about 4 m apart, sharing a common sidewalk. Alf had served in World War I, was a member of the Legion and proudly walked in the Veteran's parade displaying all of his medals. Alf was employed as manager of the local LCBO warehouse.

Alf was a bit of a character. He was very fond of LCBO products and had a permanent aroma of alcohol. He spent most of his spare time at the local Legion, swapping war stories and lies about the past. He usually arrived home, slightly inebriated and Jessie would not let Alf in the house. Alf was a fan of George Formby, an English musician who played the ukulele. Since Alf could not enter the house, he would stroll up and down our common sidewalk, playing George Formby songs on his ukulele. The fact that the performance usually occurred in the wee hours of the morning was not always appreciated. Fortunately, Alf did not sing and play the ukulele like his idol, he only played.

Alf regularly employed Mick and I on Saturday mornings to unload a freight car full of liquor at the LCBO warehouse. The car was located on a rail siding beside the warehouse and if the freight car doors did not line up with the doors of the warehouse, we had to pull the car along the track using a Badger Railway Mover. The Badger was a rail mounted cast iron pry bar that was placed under one wheel and pushed down to move the car a short distance at a time. We pushed the car along until the rail car doors lined up with the unloading doors of the warehouse. After Alf cut the seal on the car rail door, we would unload the car. Four cases at a time, stacked on a two-wheel dolly. Occasionally a case would fall or be damaged breaking a bottle inside. We were never held responsible. Alf was in charge of opening the box to assess the damage and file a report with the supplier. Damaged boxes provided Alf with a regular free supply of liquor. Sometimes one broken bottle would be recorded as two. We were usually finished by noon, unless there was more than one freight car. The pay was good, much better than delivering magazines and newspapers. There was always enough money for a movie, a milkshake at the Lorna Doone restaurant or a hamburger at George's.

· · · · · · ·

The Lorna Doone was a restaurant on Victoria Avenue in Fort William, and it was our favorite hangout. After the Friday night movie, we would head to the Lorna Doone for a feast of French fries, milkshakes and sundaes. We also hoped to meet some members of the opposite sex while there and invite them to our booth.

We would try to stretch out our time there as long as possible, much to the exasperation of the owner, Mr. Coburn. Our American friend Dick Brace worked illegally at the restaurant, when he was courting my wife's good friend Helen.

Our next favorite restaurant was George's, conveniently located on Arthur Street across from McKellar Hospital. It was also on the way home from the downtown movies. George was from Greece and knew how to cook the best hamburger that you have ever tasted. It was loaded with fried onions and a secret sauce that he ladled on. George wore an ill-fitting, poorly matched toupee that he had probably bought from the Eaton's catalogue A chef's hat would have been much more suitable.

· · · · · · ·

I could not throw a football very well, but I could run, and I could catch. I really envied my friend Mick, who could throw a big, long spiral. When I was in Grade Nine, I made the football team as a running end. We practiced in fair weather and foul. Our quarter-back could really throw the ball well. My great day came when we played the Fort William Vocational Institute team. They were bigger but not better. They did have one big guy, who carried the ball on a buck. I was playing defense that day and to encourage my teammates, I would yell "Get the bucker, get the bucker." The referee unfortunately heard it differently. He blew the whistle and was going to throw me out of the game for swearing. He thought that I had said "Get the bugger." The quarter-back came to the rescue and explained to the referee that he had heard me incorrectly.

· · · · · · ·

I was not a Cub, but I did join the local Boy Scout troop. I was in the Crow patrol along with Bob Corbett, who later became my brother-in-law when he married my wife's sister. Our scout troop was sponsored by St. Paul's Anglican Church and we met on Tuesday night, once a week, in the church basement. Our patrol leader was Donald Houston and our scoutmaster was Bill Ellard. We would retrieve wooden staves marked with the insignia of our patrol and then line up to recite the Boy Scout creed.

On my honor, I promise to do my duty to God and the Queen

To help other people at all times and to obey the scout law.

We would then salute with our right hand using two fingers. If you met another scout, you use your left hand to handshake, so that your right hand was free to salute. It was confusing for left-handed people. We would then line up for inspection of our uniforms. We had to be meticulous about our uniforms and have our shoes polished, kerchiefs properly knotted and shirts clean and pressed. During the meeting, we would play games, gather around a pretend campfire, qualify for proficiency badges and discuss the next field trip. Collecting and displaying your proficiency badges was a matter of honor and eventually I was qualified to become a Queen's Scout. Scouting has been an important part of my life. In the 1950s, I was elected president of the Guelph Boy Scout Association and in the 2000s as a Master Gardener, I taught Cubs how to obtain their gardening badges. Scouting also played an important part in the life of my eldest son, who has taken an active role in scouting activities in Duncan, B.C. for many years.

· · · · · · ·

I delivered the Valedictory Address when our Grade Thirteen class graduated from the Fort William Collegiate Institute. I have no idea what I said or why I was chosen. I had friends who were better scholars. I think that it was because my English teacher and mentor made the choice, and I was the better orator. My parents were in attendance, of course but my one disappointment was that my girlfriend and future wife could not be there. Perhaps she was not invited?

· · · · · · ·

I did some pretty reckless things as a teenager and one of them was skijoring. Skijoring was a winter sport developed by the Norwegians, where a person on cross-country skis is pulled by a team of dogs while holding on to a rope. Over a period of time, it morphed into being pulled by a horse or a motorized vehicle. In my case this was a period of time before snowmobiles appeared, so the family car was used to pull the skier along the side of the road. We usually chose a road with little traffic and snow on the surface. The road to Chippewa Park and the Fort William Golf and Country Club were favorites. In the winter there was always plenty of snow cover on the roads because salt doesn't work very well at low temperatures. We would tie two long ropes to the bumper of the car and the car would take off at five to ten kph, pulling the two skiers. That was reasonably safe, but boring, so we would slalom or zigzag up and along the snowbanks at the side of the road. The trouble was that we could not see any obstructions coming up, such as ploughed private driveways, mailboxes and trees. Collisions and spills were inevitable. Skiers were cautioned not to wrap the rope around their wrist so that it would release. Fortunately, no one was hurt.

· · · · · · ·

Bumper hitching was a variation of skijoring and was usually carried out in the city without the driver's knowledge. You merely grabbed the bumper of the car and slid along in the snow using your feet as skis. Variations involved being pulled by the streetcar. This sport was far more dangerous than skijoring. You could easily hit a bare spot and tumble into traffic coming from the other direction. Once again, no one was injured.

· · · · · · ·

I am not sure why the Scots invented the bagpipes, and I am sure that many wished that they never existed. This was particularly true if one of the neighbor's children was learning to play and was forced to practice outside the house. This was a great relief for the parents involved, but not for the neighbors who were forced to participate.

My friends Rod MacLennan, Neil Black and Helen Brace all played in the Fort William Pipe Band., which was organized by Rod's father. There was an assortment of drummers who joined in creating a glorious sound. The band actually did put on a good show and usually led the parade. My friends continued to play the pipes throughout their adult lives.

· · · · · · ·

My parents used to grow sweet peas in our backyard. There was one row located beside the driveway, and the sweet peas climbed up a chicken wire fence. The sweet peas liked the location and grew profusely. My father always wore a suit to the office, and he owned a clip-on boutonniere which he would fill with water, insert a sweet pea and then head off to his job at the Great Lakes Paper Company. I have never been able to grow sweet peas with any success. Perhaps it was the manure that they used as fertilizer?

Which brings to mind the saying: "She was only the farmer's daughter. But all the horsemen knew her." Say it fast!

· · · · · · ·

We had raspberry bushes and a rhubarb patch in the backyard, but we never grew any fresh vegetables, such as beans, radishes, beets and carrots. I was introduced to vegetable gardening at the age of ten. It was 1940 and Canadians were encouraged to plant Victory Gardens in order to raise food and help the war effort. Many men had left the farms to join up and there was a shortage of fresh vegetables. My garden was located on some vacant property behind my friend Mick's house. The city had arranged for the fields to be ploughed. Furrows were cut with a horse-drawn plough to turn the sod. There was no harrowing. It was left to us to attack the sod with a hoe and a rake. It was tough work in the first year. I planted onions, radishes, carrots, beets, wax beans, tomatoes and peas.

Unfortunately, my garden was located in some low ground and regularly flooded during the spring rains. I can remember digging a pit to collect the water in a pail and haul it away. Later in my adult years, I always had a vegetable garden, where I would grow all of my old favorites. Fortunately, horses and ploughs were replaced by rototillers. My gardens were also always located on high well-drained ground. I had learned my lesson.

Radio was a constant source of entertainment in the 1940s. One of the popular methods of advertising was by short catchy rhymes or song. Several come to mind:

Burn Murphy's coal it's the best, it's the best,
You'll feel as warm as a bird in its. nest,
When you need heat, there is nothing can beat,
Murphy's coal, Murphy's coal, it's the best.

Brylcreem, a little dab will do ya
Brylcreem, you'll look so debonair,
Brylcreem, the gals will pursue ya,
Simply put a little in your hair

Come round any old time, and make yourself at home,
Put your feet on the mantle shelf,
Open the cupboard and help yourself,
I don't care if your friends have left you all alone,
Rich or poor, just knock on the door and make yourself at home.

. . . .

We listened to radio shows on a regular basis, Some of my favorites included Abbott and Costello, The Aldrich Family, Amos 'n' Andy and shows featuring Bing Crosby, Bob Hope, Fred Allen, Jack Benny, Red Skelton, Milton Berle and Perry Como. In high school I used to hurry home at lunch to hear The Happy Gang sponsored by Colgate-Palmolive Soap. I liked the songs and the jokes. I can remember the introduction.

Knock! Knock! Knock!
Knock! Knock! Knock!
Who's there?
It's The Happy Gang!
Wel-l-l-l, come on ii-i-i-i-in!

And their opening song.

Here we are, the Happy Gang is here,
Here we are, how do you do,
Here we are to take away your troubles,
With a song, a melody or two
Use Palmolive Soap daily in your shower,
Then you'll start each morning with a bang!

JUST ME

Won't you join us when we sing and shout
We're Palmolive's Happy Gang!

Many of the original Happy Gang cast went on to become quite famous and host their own shows. I think one of the most successful radio ditties was the production of Lifebuoy Health Soap for the elimination of body odor or B.O. On the radio, the ad was introduced with the sound of a sinister sounding foghorn indicating that B.O. was noticeable. Once the foghorn sounded, a nasty sounding "Beeeee Ohhhhhh" was heard. People got the message, "That Lifebuoy really stops B.O." The Dick Tracy comic strip had characters titled B.O. Plenty, his wife Gravel Gertie and daughter Sparkle Plenty

· · · · · · ·

We always celebrated the New Year by going to the Royal Edward Hotel. The men all wore tuxedos, and the ladies wore full-length dresses with all of their finery. I wore my suit. We had a private room prior to the formalities of the dining room, and the men usually had a few drinks to prepare themselves for the festivities to follow. Sometimes they had one too many drinks, because there was always wine and champagne at dinner. During the dinner, the ritual was to ask the ladies to dance. This was the part that I hated. I had to dance first with my mother and then with my sister, followed by any other young ladies in the dining room. I seriously thought of faking a sprained ankle before the event.

· · · · · · ·

We had a ping-pong table in the basement and so did one of my friends. After the Friday night movies, we would end up at either house to play either singles or doubles. Hot chocolate, milkshakes and fudge, provided the necessary energy.

Ping-pong is basically played like tennis. The serve is very important, and I developed a wicked serve which was hard to return. My father liked to play and was very good. He also liked to win and as my serve improved, his joy of playing with me diminished.

. . . .

The high school dance was held in the gymnasium of Fort William Collegiate Institute. The music was usually provided by a disk jockey playing records on a gramophone. There was always a teacher present to monitor our behavior, and to make sure there were no party crashers or liquor consumed. This was an era when everyone had a dance card, which listed the girls that you had invited to dance and who had accepted. You always tried to have the last dance with your current crush. We also had Stag and Hen dances. In a Stag and Hen dance, the girls sat or stood on one side of the school gymnasium and the boys sat or stood on the other side. Music was provided by a disc jockey who would announce that the next set was either a boy's tag or a girl's tag. If it was a boy's tag, each boy would walk across the dance floor and tag a dance partner. During the dance set, any boy, who had been left on the sidelines could cut in and tag a boy who was dancing and dance with his girl. The boy who was tagged could either stay on the dance floor and tag someone else or retire to the sidelines. Girl's tag worked the same way, resulting in a real mixing of the participants and a chance for everyone to dance. I have disliked dancing all my life and I was finally saved from the dance floor with the development of my CMT disease and my inability to walk or balance properly.

. . . .

I met my wife Pat at a high school Stag and Hen dance in 1946. This was an open dance that anyone could attend. Pat was attending the Fort William Vocational School at the time and had come with her friend Helen. I think that Helen had an interest in my friend Jim Burrow at the time and she convinced Pat to come with her. I cannot remember who tagged who, but I do remember, ending up with Pat. I was immediately smitten. It was the beginning of a relationship that would last a lifetime. She was a good dance partner and always followed my strange dance steps. I was a terrible

JUST ME

dancer. My dancing has not improved with time. I love music and have rhythm in my heart, but it never reaches my feet. Both my sister and my mother tried to teach me how to fox trot, polka and waltz, but I would get them all mixed up. In desperation, I invented the McCavour two-step which I used for all occasions. Fortunately, Pat caught on and I was saved. She always followed my lead, no matter how erratic. I walked Pat home that night, taking the darkest and longest route. It was the beginning of a long relationship.

· · · · · · ·

My parents were very good about loaning me their car, with the condition that I brought it home before midnight. On one occasion, after a late-night date with Pat, I drove the car down the back lane so that I could park it in the backyard. I decided to turn off the lights, which normally shone into my parent's upstairs bedroom window, without waking them up. It was pitch dark, and the car overshot the parking lot and bumped into the house with a large bang, waking everyone inside. I was grounded for a month. The game of bridge was very popular in the 40s and remains popular today among my peer group. My parents, my grandmother and their friends were all avid bridge players. My sister and her husband were excellent bridge players. Ely Culbertson was the bridge guru of the time and he wrote books and articles about how to play Contract Bridge. Lacking bridge players at home, my sister and I were taught how to play by our parents using Culbertson guidelines. All of my teen friends played bridge and the game was pursued during my high school and my university years. In the forties, fifties and sixties, Charles Goren was the bridge expert. His method of point-counting and bidding was a great improvement over Culbertson's clumsy honor-trick method. There have been some changes in recent years, including five card majors and week two bids, but basically it is still Goren. Currently my wife uses a bridge game titled The Baron on her computer and also belongs to a ladies' bridge club. We both play in Probus bridge events and read and discuss the Toronto Star bridge game.

· · · · · · ·

In public school, punishment for minor misdemeanors such as talking, passing notes or giggling was rewarded by having to stay after school and clean the chalk brushes, while major misdemeanors, such as fighting, swearing or lying, required a strapping. It is rather interesting to note that seventy-five years after getting the strap from my Grade Eight teacher. The Liberal Government is considering repealing Section Forty-three of the Criminal Code of Canada, which protects parents and to a lesser extent, teachers, who use reasonable physical force against children. The abolitionists and advocates of Justice for Children and Youth argued that in a society, where we don't hit people, we also don't hit children. I can recall being threatened with a spanking or a strapping during my youth, but it never came to pass. My time did come, however, in Grade Eight. My punishment was for teasing Annis Ferrier and passing a note around the class, calling her Anus Ferrier. She had retaliated by stabbing my left knee with a pencil and marking me with a permanent carbon tattoo. It is still visible today. In the commotion that followed, we were escorted to the cloakroom and interrogated. I pleaded that I had made a simple spelling mistake and had been wounded as a consequence. Annis pleaded that my remarks were libelous, embarrassing and caused great mental anguish. She later became a lawyer. The teacher ruled that I was guilty and much to Annis's delight, I received five straps on each hand. In high school Annis changed her name to Nan.

· · · · · · ·

We exchanged Valentine cards in public school, but not in high school. In my younger years, we made our own cards by cutting them out of a pre-printed book. The cards were then put in a Valentine box and on Valentine day, the cards were distributed to each student. The love message on the card and the source of the card were not important. The important thing was the number of cards you received. Some cards were mysteriously signed, "Guess Who?" For some of the students, it was upsetting and humiliating to receive only one or two cards. Some kids cheated and stuffed the box with self-addressed cards to ensure their popularity.

JUST ME

As time went on, the quality of the cards improved, and the message and sex of the sender became important. We were maturing. In high school the Valentine box was put away and replaced by Canada Post. In retrospect, I think the Valentine box was a bad idea.

· · · · · · ·

There is a great advantage in having a long telephone cord. The telephone at my home was located at the foot of the stairs leading to the second floor. Making a telephone call was a public event, because your voice travelled a long distance. I did not want anyone to know when I was talking to my girlfriend Pat. With the long cord, I found that I could sit in the front hall closet and close the door for privacy. My parents had trouble finding he phone. Children of today do not fully appreciate the privacy of wireless phones.

· · · · · · ·

In my public-school days, the new basement room beneath the den was used as a playroom. When I went to high school., it became my study. Some of my friends were able to work in a busy library or with a group of friends. I preferred to work by myself with no distractions, and still do.

The room originally had a bare concrete floor, and my father hired a man from the GLP Company to build a wooden floor in the room. I was given the job of sanding the hardwood floor and did a good job except at the edges, where I allowed the sander to run too long leaving a groove in the wood. It was a constant reminder for me of screwing up my first finishing job.

My parents presented me with a huge oak roll-top desk with an abundance of drawers, where I could hide my treasures. I loved the desk and hated to part with it when I went to Queen's University. My nephew, Ian inherited the desk.

· · · · · · ·

My father always bought Chrysler cars from our neighbor, who was a dealer. I had learned how to drive and got my license at the age of sixteen. My father was very good about loaning me the car and I am afraid that I abused the privilege. I frequently called on Pat and we would go out for a drive. It was mid- winter. We were driving over in Port Arthur one evening circling Boulevard Lake while it was snowing. Pat was driving and having a hard time, because it was difficult to see. I decided to drive and got out of the car to change places. I found myself up to my boots in slush. I could see open water ahead. We were in the middle of Boulevard Lake. Pat had taken a wrong turn in the storm, ending up on an ice road. It was used to cut large blocks of ice to be stored and sold the following summer for ice-box refrigerators. It was a close call. The car, with Shirley and I in it, could have ended up at the bottom of the lake. Once, while taking another driving lesson on Mission Island. Pat drove the car into the ditch. We survived and the car survived, but the oil pan was damaged in the process. Courtship could be damaging.

One weekend Pat and I drove the car down to visit our newly wedded friends the Braces in Minneapolis, Minnesota. Whether by plan or necessity. Pat and I had to share the same bed in the guest bedroom. I didn't get much sleep that night, but Pat retained her virginity. The Braces did not believe her. On another occasion, I took Pat and the Chrysler partridge hunting. We parked the car on a country road and walked down the road looking for partridge. I had a twenty-two rifle, loaded with short cartridges, rather than a larger rifle that fired buckshot. My gun required good marksmanship. At the end of the day, we had not even seen a partridge and were walking back to the car, when one appeared in the middle of the road. I took careful aim, fired and missed. The next day my father presented me with a lead slug, which he had found at the bottom of a shattered taillight.

I cannot remember ever paying for gas or for the damage done to the car. My father was too forgiving. I was spoiled.

· · · · · · · ·

From the age of fifteen, I always had a summer job. My father believed in the work ethic and I was not to be spared. The jobs were secured from various friends, clients and contractors, who were associated with my father. One summer I worked for Clayton Construction demolishing a temporary grain storage building that had been used during the war to store unsold grain. There were concrete conveyor tunnels, running down the middle of the structure, which had been used for removing the grain. The vertical tunnel walls were the toughest. I weighed about sixty-five kg at the time and had to hold a twenty-seven kg pneumatic jackhammer in a horizontal position as the chisel rotated and impacted the concrete. It was tough, noisy, dusty and exhausting, During the same summer, my friend Mick worked at Northern Engineering making bomb casings on a lathe.

Our neighbor Jack Irwin employed me at the Western Grain Elevator unloading grain cars from western Canada. This was another tough job. Unloading was done by two men who were tethered together with a harness. When one man with an empty bucket entered the railcar, he would pull and help the other man with a loaded bucket out of the car. Jack and most of the men chewed tobacco and went around with a plug of tobacco in their cheek because of the continuous dust in the air. With no spittoons handy, they would spit anywhere, including in the grain. I was always suspicious about the origin of the brown bread that I ate.

I spent another summer at the Western Grain Elevator bagging barley flour on the night shift from four to twelve. It had to be the dirtiest job I ever had. I would stand in front of a spout hanging from the ceiling with my bag held open to catch the falling barley flour. I would then tie and stack my bag. We worked in a cloud of dust and wore face masks. At the end of the shift, I would head for home on the streetcar completely covered with dust, looking like a zombie. There were small balls of barley paste in the corners of my eyes.

My father thought that my summers would be better spent working in construction. He lined up a job for me working for George Houston. This was not an office job. Houston had a contract for an addition to the McKellar General Hospital and I started off connecting the rebar with tie wire in the concrete forms. I also spent time shoveling sand and gravel into a concrete mixer. Ready-mix concrete did not appear until the sixties. On occasion, when they were short on crew, I would push a wheelbarrow full of concrete up a ramp to fill the empty forms. That job didn't last after I dumped the wheelbarrow. I also learned about the contractor's trick of adding an extra bag cement to the mixer when Scott, the architect, appeared to take a concrete test cylinder. The concrete always tested over strength. When I had my own engineering company, I never announced my arrival on the job to take a test cylinder. The foreman on the hospital job was Sam Waski. Sam was a charming man with a big grin hat exposed a mouth with half of the teeth missing. We would sit down and have lunch together, discussing everything from politics to construction problems. Sam hated paperwork and assigned me the job of checking all the time sheets and subcontractor bills. It was better than working on the concrete mixer. The following summer, I worked for Houston, building the Port Arthur incinerator. There was a control building on the site and the chimney had become plugged with debris during construction. Removal was difficult and I suggested to Sam that we could light a fire and burn it out. The fire wouldn't catch, so Sam decided to pour a little gasoline on the debris. It worked. Sam lit a match and blew the contents of the flue into the air, along with the top of the chimney. It was not a great idea.

In retrospect, my father's work ethic lesson was successful. I carried the ethic into my later life.

. . . .

Every generation has a clothes fad that teens slavishly follow. My teenage children would take a perfectly good pair of jeans and antique the with bleach. Wear was encouraged and the holier the better. Worn out jeans were treasured and not trashed. My grandsons paraded in baggy oversize jeans with the belt line worn at the bum line. Fortunately, we all grow older, and our dress code begins to conform. Diamond socks were the male fad of my day, sometimes enhanced with a diamond pattern sweater. For some reason the socks and sweaters were not available in Canada and we would trek down to Duluth, Minnesota to make our purchases, I had a good collection, but both socks and fads wear out. By my twenties, I had graduated to a monochromatic sock design. I did however wear a red and white diamond sweater That lasted for years. We also had zoot suits in my day, consisting of bell-bottom trousers with a watch chain, dangling from the belt to the knee, then back to a side pocket and pleated coats with padded shoulders. I did not approve or wear a zoot suit. Pat had also created a cable knit sweater for me, which was great, except for the-off-the shoulder neckline.

· · · · · · ·

Almost all teens get acne, and I was no exception. Mine persisted for five years. It happens when an oily substance called sebum clogs your pores. Pimples usually pop up on the face, neck, chest and shoulders. My acne was on the side of my cheeks. Although it was not a serious health risk, it can damage self esteem at a time of life that you want to look your best. I had an assortment of blackheads and whiteheads that I would regularly squeeze, causing further aggravation. Some turned into angry pustules. I scrubbed, cleaned and tried various ointments and masking powders, only making matters worse. My parents finally intervened and sent me to Dr. Ferrier, the local dermatologist. He treated ne with X-rays, the popular cure at the time. It was found fifty years later that the incidence of thyroid, breast and skin cancer increased if you had a past history of radiation treatments. When I was being treated for basal cell carcinoma, one of the questions was, "Have you had X-ray treatments for acne?" Fortunately, I survived.

· · · · · · ·

I have been blessed with a variety of good teachers who have enriched my life.

At Fort William Collegiate Institute, Grant Shane was principal, Christine Tilden taught English, Lefty Cornell and Harry Moran taught Math, Sadie Miller taught French, while R. B. Inkster taught Phys. Ed. and Sex Ed. My home room was with Pat Scollie. Elmer Huff, who roomed at my friend's house, was another great teacher.

At the Lakehead Technical Institute, I enjoyed my English teacher Alex Ross, and Harold Braun, who taught Physics. Harold went on to become a president of Lakehead University and co-authored a book on the Lakehead University with my brother-in-law Bill Tamblyn.

At Queen's University, I liked Professor Harkness in Physics and Professors Brooks and Lash in Structural Design.

....

When I was ten or eleven, I reluctantly attended Wesley United Church with my parents every Sunday morning, except in the summer when I got two months off. I don't think that my parents were very religious and only attended because it was considered the best thing to do. I can't remember ever discussing religion with my parents or exploring the "Is there a God?" subject or Trinitarian versus Unitarian beliefs. I just attended Sunday after Sunday.

Churches were very cliquey. All of the close friends of my parents attended the United Church, while other friends attended other churches. I can't remember any close friends of the family who were Roman Catholic, Jewish, Oriental or Colored. My parents were definitely White, Anglo-Saxon Protestants, otherwise known as WASPs. All of the McCavour clan were members of the United Church and had originally been Methodists. The McCavour family attended the Centenary Queen Square United Church in Saint John, New Brunswick, in the early 1900s. My Aunt Alicia and Aunt Annie continued to support the church with donations and the installation of a stained-glass memorial window. Church attendance deteriorated and the church was eventually sold in 1966.

Our Sunday ritual was to walk to church, which was quite unusual for my father, who avoided exercise on the remaining six days of the week. "There is nothing better than a brisk morning walk," he would enthuse, while the rest of us prayed for rain. My mother and grandmother did not share my father's religious fervor and were often slow to get ready, necessitating the use of the car. Reverend James was the minister at the time and Arthur K. Putland (nicknamed Putty) was the organist and choir director. My sister Mugs sang soprano in the choir. After marrying Bill Tamblyn, she converted to Anglicanism. My father contended that she would eventually become a follower of the Pope. We always sat in the same pew in the second row of the balcony, center right. There was no nameplate or dedication on the pew, but everyone knew that this is where the McCavour family sat. All of our friends occupied similar pews and commanded the same respect.

The service began at eleven and the first half hour was devoted to song, scripture reading, announcements and collection of the offering . The next half hour was torture, including a sermon and never-ending prayers. I did not pay much attention to the service, but I sang the hymns enthusiastically and always enjoyed the children's story.

I also pent a good deal of time studying an older man, who sat in the front row of the balcony on the right. His clothing was shabby, and he certainly was not very good looking with a few wisps of hair and a permanent stubble on his chin. He needed a good shave and a haircut. Most interesting to me was a large lump, the size of a plum, on the side of his face. I would study this lump intently, speculating what might have caused it and what it might be. I always looked forward each Sunday when I could check out the size of the lump, to see if it had changed. This went on for years and the lump never changed. Then one Sunday he was not in his customary spot. I looked around the other pews and he wasn't there. Maybe he had moved or switched to another church or even died because of the lump. He just disappeared. "Thank goodness he's gone," mother commented. "He certainly didn't belong in our church." My mother had forgotten that the House of the Lord serves all. The nice thing about being a kid, was that we didn't have to listen to the sermon. After the second verse of the second hymn,, we would escape to Sunday school in the church basement. Mr. Buckley, a schoolteacher during the week, also functioned as the Sunday school superintendent. He would deliver the bible reading for the day and we would then have a round of children's hymns. I can still sing and recite them from memory.

Jesus loves me, this I know,
For the Bible tells me so,
Little ones to him belong,
We are weak and he is strong.

Yes, Jesus loves me,
Yes, Jesus loves me,
Yes, Jesus loves me,
The Bible tells me so.

And another favorite:

Jesus bids us shine
With a clear pure light,
Like a burning candle,
Shining in the night.
In this world of darkness,
Jesus makes us shine,
You in your small corner
And I in mine.

Then we would break off into small groups and discuss the Bible reading. Frankly, I did not learn a thing at Sunday school. My mind was elsewhere. But at least I had escaped the sermon.

· · · · · · ·

In my teen years, religious salvation came when an older student named Jack Nugent suggested to the minister that the teenage male members of the congregation would be more enriched if they attended a special Bible study group that he would organize. The minister liked the plan. The Wesley Bible Study Group was formed and it became quite popular. Jack quickly re-identified it as a club and it was rechristened as the Tuscarora Club. It was an excellent way for us to escape the sermon. I have no idea who came up with the name Tuscarora. It is actually the name of a native American tribe, which was part of the Iroquois family and lived in North Carolina, New York and the Great Lakes area.

Jack suggested that the club should have officers and I was elected president, along with a vise president, secretary and treasurer. Minutes of the meeting were duly recorded.

Jack would pick an interesting story from the Bible and then ask us what we thought about it. Did it occur? Was it possible? What was the message? And so on. That would last for about 15 minutes and then we would spend the rest of the time socializing and planning a non-church event.

Jack paid a great deal of attention to me in the years that followed. He was six years older, and I took a great pride in his friendship. When Jack joined the air force, he began writing long letters about every aspect of his life in the Air Training Program. He showered me with badges and air-force insignia. In the course of the war, he would write hundreds of letters, which I dutifully read and collected. Did my parents like the relationship? No. My mother thought he was weird, and my father thought he was a pervert.

At the end of the war Jack went back to university to compete his education in journalism., but he always kept in touch. By the time I was dating Pat, Jack made a point of visiting Bryan's Department Store where she was working to check her out. Our relationship cooled after that. When my friends and I all chose Queen's University in Kingston, Jack got a job working for the Kingston Whig Standard newspaper. He made a point of getting together with us on weekends. Following my marriage, the umbilical cord with Jack was cut. I never heard from him again.

Was my relationship with Jack normal? No. Was Jack a pedophile? No. Pedophiles are normally interested in pre-puberty children and not teenagers. He had many of the character traits of a pedophile, providing me with excessive attention, and showering me with gifts to gain friendship and respect. But he never went beyond those boundaries. Following our group to Kingston was not coincidental. Jack was looking for a suitable companion. During the ten years that I knew Jack, not once did he make a sexual move. Summing it up, I think that Jack was a homosexual, hunting for a mate. He never found one.

· · · · · · · ·

My sex education was anecdotal in my early years, with information passed on by my older friends. I studied the underwear and brassiere ads in the Eaton's catalogue, speculating on what lay hidden beneath. I subscribed to *Sunbathing Magazine*, which was mailed in a plain brown wrapper and depicted naked men and women playing volleyball and other sports. *Playboy Magazine* would not appear until the 1960s. When we were at a friend's house, he would show us medical books on the human anatomy from his father's medical library. They were not very exciting. By the time I reached high school, our boy's physical education teacher attempted to give us a course on sex education, complete with pull-down diagrams of our reproductive organs. Much to our relief and contrary to religious teaching at the time, the teacher explained that masturbation was normal and not harmful. He also laughingly assured us that we would not grow hair on our hands, but that we should always carry a condom, if we decided to explore the matter further with a girl. I stored the box in my sock drawer. The condoms were never used, but I could always brag, that I had them handy. I think that our teacher preferred to teach us about basketball and rugby.

The classes were short and there was no question period.

· · · · · · ·

Scollies was conveniently located on Catherine Street near the Fort William Collegiate Institute. They produced ice cream bricks, chocolate-coated Revels, cones and tubs of bulk ice cream. We would walk over at lunchtime for a cone and sometimes skipped a class for a treat. One year, Pat Scollie, a member of the Scollie family was my home room teacher. Unfortunately, I did not attend any of his classes. Pat was a friendly man with a bald head and a big smile. He was an excellent teacher.

· · · · · · ·

Doug Bryan lived at the end of Cuthbertson place, where it intersects with Selkirk Avenue. The Bryan house was the biggest house on the street and accommodated a family of four children and two, adults. There was an apartment in the house that was rented out. Oddly enough I never stepped foot in the house.

Doug was one year younger and attached himself to Mick and me. He would play can-the-can, football and hockey with us, but he was always the last to be chosen to join the team. He was always the odd man out.

When I attended high school. Mick and Doug would knock on our back door and then crowd into the kitchen for a cookie or a muffin, while I dressed. You get hungry after walking a short distance. Then the three of us would head off to school.

Doug's father and uncle owned Bryan's Department Store. It was the second biggest store in Fort William after Chapple's. In addition, Mr. Bryan owned many apartments in Fort William, and it was Doug's job to collect the monthly rents. Having nothing better to do, I would tag along. We used our bicycles to get around because the apartments were scattered throughout the city. One Saturday morning we were making the collection rounds and I darted across Victoria Avenue from between two parked cars. I was run down by an oncoming automobile. The next thing I remember was waking up in our bathtub, which was half full of bloody water. I had a concussion and multiple cuts and abrasions, but no broken bones. The bike had been totaled and my parents assured me that I would get a new one. They were just glad I was alive.

One morning Doug did not show up at the back door. Later that day, I checked with his mom, who reported that Doug was sick with stomach cramps. He did not show up the next day and his mom reported that Doug was now seriously ill at McKellar Hospital with a ruptured appendix. There were no miracle drugs or antibiotics in those days and Doug died of peritonitis poisoning.

I was devastated and did not know how to deal with my grief. When my friend Billy Mahon had died of leukemia, it was expected. His family were Christian Scientists and did not believe in the practice of medicine. Doug should not have died. The doctor had waited too long to remove the appendix before it ruptured. I talked about Doug's death tearfully with my high school teacher, Miss Tilden. She suggested that I could write about it. I went home the night before Doug's funeral and wrote a poem, which was read at his funeral. It was titled "A Friend of Ours."

A friend of ours has left us, On a
trip without an end. He caught
God's bus a while ago; In a
minute was round the bend.

Gone from our sight, like the lightning's flash
Out of all earthly view,
He's turned a curve on the road to Heaven,
To be lost to me and to you.

He is lost to our sight; but the voice of his soul
Remains with us forever;
Fond memories of his speech and smile,
Linger on, forgotten never.

The poem was first published in the school yearbook and has been republished many times since. I had always written and still write limericks, but this was my first serious poem. Later in my life I would publish a book titled Poems and Songs – Old and New, which became a Bestseller.

. . . .

I attended the Fort William Collegiate Institute or F.W.C.I., which was an academic school, preparing students to go on to university or college. At that time, it was a five-year term, which was later changed to a four-year term in the 1960s. My wife Pat, on the other hand, attended the Fort William Vocational Institute, which prepared students for a trade or vocation. It was a great five years for me. I looked forward to attending school. I remember and can still recite the two school yells.

First.
Boom-a-lacka, Boom-a-lacka, Bow-wow-wow;
Chick-a-lacka, Chick-a-lacka, Chow, chow, chow;
Boom-a-lacka-bic, Chick-a-lack-a chick,
Fort William Collegiate, Ric-rac-ric!

JUST ME

And second:
Blue and Gold, Blue and Gold; We are
the people. We are told. Razzle, dazzle
ziz-boom -bah, Fort William Collegiate,
Rah-rah-rah! . . .

    Silly lyrics, yes, but nevertheless they are unforgettable. I participated in many of the extra-curricular activities, as a guard on the football team, member of the curling club, member of the boxing and wrestling club and vice-president of the literary society. I acted in school plays, helped run social events, wrote poems and limericks, was editor of the school yearbook and class valedictorian. I think it was a big fish in a little pond situation; university for me was an ego leveler. Competition was much tougher.

· · · · · · ·

Muriel Hutchings was the first girl the first girl that I dated in high school. She was a good friend of Mick's girlfriend, Audrey Kennedy. I guess that is how we met. We were both in the same grade. Muriel was very petite, very pretty and very shy. Dating was a learning curve for both of us. Dates in those days usually occurred on Friday nights and involved a movie and a visit to the Lorna Doone restaurant after the show for a milkshake and an ice-cream sundae. The boy usually paid the bill, so dates were costly and infrequent. We walked home slowly with some exploratory hand holding, just in time for her twelve-p.m. curfew. You do not kiss on a first date.

    Muriel and I drifted apart in the years that followed, but my friend Mick went on to marry his high school girlfriend, Audrey Kennedy.

· · · · · · ·

Norm and Nora Jenkins were my parents' best friends. They visited back and forth and shared dinners, picnics, travels and holidays. Norm owned one of the local funeral homes in Fort William. The business was located in a two-story building on Syndicate Avenue. The Jenkins family lived on the second floor with their daughter, Gayda and their grandmother Duffy.

I was allowed to visit the chapel and the casket display room but was never allowed in the mortuary. Since there was an eight-year difference in age between Gayda and me, I could not talk her into sneaking into the mortuary to see the dead bodies.

There was a large neon sign that Norm had erected below a second-floor window at the front of the building, proclaiming Jenkins Funeral Home in flashing red lights. One day their cat ventured out of the open window and onto the sign, causing a short circuit and electrocuting itself in the process. Much to the amusement of the community, the sign now read Jenkins Fun Home. Coincidentally Jenkins' main competitor was named Everest. The local news media had a ball with the two names.

· · · · · · · ·

Although barbecuing meat is quite common today, it was relatively new in the 1950s. My sister and brother-in-law had a cottage at Birch Beach on the shores of Thunder Bay. They had invited the family for a birthday celebration and a steak dinner. The steaks were sitting on the kitchen counter and their dog grabbed one and ran away. We took off in pursuit and the dog finally dropped the steak on the road. We decided that the steak would be edible after cooking as long as we washed off the sand from the road and nobody would be the wiser.

The barbecue party continued, and the steaks were cooked and served. Everyone thought that they were delicious, and nobody was the wiser about the stolen meat. We had no idea who had ended up with the stolen steak until I asked Grandma Baird If she had enjoyed her barbecued steak. She said it tasted a little gritty.

· · · · · · ·

My brother-in-law was the proud owner of a 1947 Hillman Minx Mark 1 drop-dead coupé. It was his pride and joy, and in an irrational moment, he decided to loan it to me to pick up my date. I picked up Pat and she was quite impressed. I don't know whatever possessed me to take my brother-in-law's Hillman Minx and then drive it forty-eight kilometres to Amethyst

Harbor. Nor do I know what possessed me to drive the car around Judge's cottage, which sat on a barren rock overlooking Thunder Bay. It was an absolutely stupid thing to do and although I refilled the gas tank, I could not change the ninety-six-kilometre reading on the odometer. My brother-in-law was furious. It was my first and last use of the Hillman Minx.

· · · · · · · ·

September 15, 1948 was a new day, a great day. It was my first day as a student at the newborn Lakehead Technical Institute in Port Arthur and the beginning of a fifty-year engineering career. The idea for Technical Institutes had emerged after the demise of the veteran training program. In Northern Ontario there was a need for trained forestry technicians, mining technicians and technologists. In other Ontario locations, the textile and other manufacturing industries were looking for trained graduates. Ryerson Institute in Toronto, the Provincial Institute for Textiles in Hamilton and the Lakehead Technical Institute all came into being. Each of the births was difficult. In the twin cities the never-ending rivalry between Fort William and Pot Arthur, plus a lack of funds was only solved when the Thunder Bay Lumber Company stepped forward with an offer of property on Cumberland Avenue in Port Arthur and the erection of a temporary building that could be rented to the Institute. The first mining technology students enrolled in January 1948. Education at the Lakehead Technical Institute had begun.

It was later that year that the concept of expanding the curriculum to include a first-year university course was introduced. This required increased teaching staff, increased revenue and better use of the new space. Five full-time and two part-time teachers were added to the existing staff of two. The next problem was to sell the concept to the community and recruit the students. It was a tough sell with a new school, a fledgling staff and a tough curriculum. By September sixty students had been recruited with fourteen in First Year Arts and Science, twenty-three in Applied Science and twenty-three in Mining and Forestry Technology.

I really didn't care about the neophyte nature of the school or the teachers. I just knew that this was the beginning of a great learning experience.,

There were no bells or loudspeaker announcements to advise the commencement of class. This was not a high school. This was first-year university. Students were responsible for getting to class on time. We all unpacked our briefcases. Some were tattered and some were new. There were no schoolbags; those were for children. Backpacks would arrive decades later. Our books were all new. First-time students paid list price. On average, the books cost about forty dollars for the first year compared to a combined tuition and lab fee of sixty dollars per year. All of the graduates were shocked when our second-year university tuition skyrocketed to $225.00. LTI was definitely a bargain.

The Applied Science curriculum included Chemistry, Descriptive Geometry, English, Engineering Drawing. Engineering and Society, Algebra, Analytical Geometry, Calculus, Plane a Spherical Trigonometry, Physics, Surveying and /or Mineralogy. It was a full, plate because it had to meet the requirements of different universities.

Our school day started at 8:00 a.m. and it ended at 5:30 p.m. There was time for an evening meal with the family and some R&R followed by a few more hours of homework. I would telephone my girlfriend Pat during the week, but we only met on weekends. Distractions were limited to radio and playing 78 rpm vinyl records. There was no TV and no time for texting. They didn't exist. I satisfied myself with music by the Ink Spots and the pop songs of Bing Crosby and Frank Sinatra. We would discuss the previous night' radio performance of the Aldrich Family or Fibber McGee and Molly on the morning bus run to LTI. The new school, which had been assembled from old army huts that had been used in constructing the Alaska Highway, was functional but primitive. The heating system was unreliable and there was no air-conditioning. There was natural ventilation, however through the uninsulated cracks in the walls and the roof leaked, particularly where the huts were joined together. Pails to catch the drips were strategically located in the classrooms and in the halls. The janitor, who had grown tired of emptying the pails, cut holes in the wood floor so that the drips could flow directly into the crawl space. It was my first introduction to hydraulics.

The classes were exciting. I looked forward to every day at LTI. Mel Jackson introduced me to the slide rule and opened the door to the world of calculus. Computers had not been invented. Our English teacher, Alex Ross, achieved the impossible by getting science students to enjoy Hemingway and The Snows of Kilimanjaro, while Harold Braun introduced us to the incredible world of physics. Teachers and students were on a first name basis from day one. They were lighting a spark that fired the excitement and joy of our future careers in engineering. Why did men and women come to a remote area of Canada to teach? Where they desperate for a job? Did they love hunting and fishing? Did they like to ski? Where they escaping from something? Why did they come to LTI?

They came to LTI because they loved to teach and sow the seeds of learning in young minds and to see those seeds grow into knowledge that would mould a future life. There was joy in seeing those students mature and pupate into successful and knowledgeable young adults. It was a communicable disease that affect most teachers.

Since our Applied Science class was all male, any social interaction occurred at lunch time. A small but functional cafeteria was located at one end of the building, where you could buy French fries, hot dogs and pop. That's where we hung out during the half-hour lunch break, with hopes of meeting the fair sex. Several relationships started there, which later became lifelong partnerships. My father served on the LTI Advisory Committee and the LTI Board, when it was first founded. After his stroke, my brother-in-law, Bill Tamblyn, took over his position on the LTI Board and served continuously for fourteen years, when he was appointed as the first president of Lakehead University.

· · · · · · ·

I purchased a snipe sailboat in 1945 and spent the next four years sailing it out of Chippewa. I was somewhat bold in christening my boat after Canada's celebrated racing ship and fishing vessel, but the name stuck even after resale. A Bluenose postage stamp was issued in 1929 and the ship appears again on the back of the Canadian dime.

1945 was the beginning of the Thunder Bay Yacht Club, which included a small group of people who wanted to sail snipe sailboats. The boat required one skipper and one crew member. I had been instructed how to sail by the previous owner and the two of us participated in the Sunday races. The boat was tippy and we soon learned how to right the boat after it capsized. Sailing off Chippewa was on the windiest part of Thunder Bay and some say the coldest. I took over the job as skipper and my girlfriend Pat crewed. The true test of our romance would come when I would get up at five a.m., pick up Pat and head off to Chippewa to sand the wooden hull for the upcoming Sunday race. There were some memorable moments. On one occasion, I asked Pat to shinny up the mast to thread the main sail rope through a pulley. She made it up the mast, threaded the rope and then with our keel plate up. The boat tipped over and Pat landed in the water. Nothing was broken, including her heart. On another occasion, Pat and I were in the Sunday race to the Welcome Islands. Helen and Dick Brace were with us. Four people in a snipe is not recommended for racing purposes but winning was not on our minds. The Welcome Islands are located about ten kilometres from Chippewa Harbour and were seen as a safe haven from the storms that frequently lashed Thunder Bay. The islands are sometimes referred to as the Three Sisters. According to legend, a great Ojibway Chief had four daughters. The three older girls were cruel and haughty and were jealous of their beautiful younger sister. One day the younger sister was walking in the woods when she heard the voice of the spirit Nanibijou, asking her if she would marry his son, North Star. The sisters were jealous and plotted to kill her when she went to see North Star. They shot her with three arrows and North Star carried her to safety in the sky, The Ojibway chief was very angry with his daughters, turned them into stone and cast them into the waters of Thunder Bay. There was a brisk breeze blowing that day, but the local commodore decided that it would be safe to run the race. We were half way to the islands when the gale hit. Helen and Dick were both hiking, sitting on the windward side of the snipe, adding their weight to counteract the heeling force of the wind. Pat was also on the windward side, controlling the jib, while I controlled the rudder and the mainsail. I had never been in such a strong wind and decided to drop the mainsail and run for shelter on the Welcome Islands, using only the jib. We made it to the harbor and waited overnight with the other sailors for the storm to pass. Our parents were worried when we did not return but were assured by the club officials that we were all safe. It was quite an adventure. There was a photograph of the Bluenose moored at the Welcome Islands harbor that hung on our wall as a reminder, for many years.

On another occasion, I had decided to sail the Bluenose on a fifty-six kilometres run, from Chippewa Harbor to Amethyst Harbor. Pat and I started early in the morning, on what was to become a very memorable day. We began with a good wind and tacked our way on a zig zag course past Fort William and Port Arthur. By the time we had passed the Port Arthur Pulp and Paper Company, the breeze had picked up and we prepared ourselves for a gusty run to Amethyst. Sailing conditions for the next five hours could test our navigational skills. There were no visibility problems, but the headwind was from the northeast, blowing directly up Thunder Bay. To make forward progress against the head wind, we had to tack, zigzagging back and forth, first to the east and next to the west, doubling our length of time on the water. Our bladders were full by this time. I was able to pee in the bailing can, but much to her embarrassment, Pat had to pee in her pants. We finally made it into the safety of South Bay and Amethyst Harbor, after ten hours on the water. My sister, Mugs, was there to greet us.

· · · · · · ·

The March winter break usually meant that our gang would head off to one of the family cottages. The Birch Beach cottage or the Floral Beach cottage were the usual destinations. On one occasion we went to the Amethyst General Store, which was being operated by the Moran family at the time. All of the buildings were unheated, so sleeping bags and an ample supply of firewood were required. There were usually six or eight of us in the group. We spent our time plying poker, talking about girls, telling dirty jokes and drinking rye and ginger ale. This was my first introduction to hard liquor. I cannot remember anyone getting drunk, but the noise level increased and the quality of poker playing decreased with the consumption of rye. Alcohol would become a problem for several of the gang. I don't like rye, but I do like scotch.

· · · · · · ·

Pat's main source of income at the time was babysitting. She had a stable of clients and the best customer was the Cerruti family, who produced continuous supply f babies. I found it quite convenient to visit Pat on these occasions and we would put the time to good use, necking on the living room sofa. If the word necking is not in your vocabulary, it means kissing and embracing sexually but fully dressed. One evening, I arrived at the Cerruti house, quite excited, to announce the arrival of my nephew, Ian Tamblyn. Usually, I left before the Cerruti's returned, but on this occasion they returned early and caught us on the couch. Pat was not asked to return and was replaced by a younger sister. The good ending to this story was that we ended up babysitting Ian.

. . . .

We had absolutely no right to build a ski shack on a remote ski trail on the west side of Mount McKay. This was Indian Reservation land and we were trespassing. There were ten of us involved in this crime and our parents seemed oblivious to the fact. We built the shack from scratch, hauling the scrounged building materials up the trail from the nearby Golf Club Road. The wood frame building was about three metre by four metres, with one window. Pat made curtains for the window. There were a few chairs, a table and wood-fired stove for heat. The building was not insulated, but it did serve the purpose as a refuge and a great rendezvous spot on cold winter ski days. The local Indians tolerated our presence and broke in occasionally looking for alcohol.

. . . .